From Lilith to

Lilith Fair

From Lilith to Lilith Fair

BY BUFFY CHILDERHOSE

St. Martin's Griffin 🟰 New York

Written by Buffy Childerhose
Design and Illustration by John Rummen
Photography by:
Brian Minato, pg 112
Crystal Heald, pp xvi, 8, 12, 18, 64, 102
Mark Van S, pp 32, 78
Merri Cyr, pp 10, 13, 19, 33, 44, 45, 62, 66, 75, 86, 97, 109
Steve Jennings, pp 20, 39, 52, 76
Susan Alzner, pg 60
All other photography by the Nettmedia team: Angelique Crowther, Bob Gourley, Cathy Barrett, Jana Lynn White, Jay Daunheimer, Lane Dunlop, Vanessa Smith
Managing Editor: Cathryn France
Editors: Neil K. Guy, Katharine Perak, Cathryn France
Photo Editor: Angelique Crowther

ISBN 0-312-20173-7
First Published in Canada by Madrigal Press Ltd.
First U.S. edition
10 9 8 7 6 5 4 3 2 1

A Madrigal Press Book

This book is dedicated to Lilith, the spirit of change,
my mother Lillian and all mothers
who tell their daughters that anything is possible.

My heartfelt thanks go out to everyone involved in Lilith Fair —
especially Sarah, my publisher Cathryn France, Carl Wilson,
Alastair Duncan, all my friends and family — especially my sister
Tracey for her patience and my dad and his credit card.

A special thank you to Mo Al-Nuaimy for his editorial advice, his
continued support and all those beautiful lies he fed me.
Ana hebek, Muhanned.

Table of Contents

Foreword by Sarah McLachlan   ix
Introduction   I
Prologue   7
Chapter One: Genesis   9
Chapter Two: The Dream – The Reality   2I
Chapter Three: Musical Mentors   53
Chapter Four: The Multimedia is the Message   6I
Chapter Five: The Media's Response   65
Chapter Six: Retrospective   77
Chapter Seven: A New Eden   II3
Index: I24

Historical Profiles
Artemisia Gentileschi   I6
Countess Ada Lovelace   24
E. Pauline Johnson (Tekahionwake)   28
Elizabeth Cady Stanton   36
Emma Goldman   40
Hannah Senesh   48
Hildegarde of Bingen   56
Hypatia   68
Lise Meitner   72
Mary Wollstonecraft   80
Murasaki Shukibu   88
Nellie McClung   92
Rani Lakshmibai   I00
Rosa Parks   I04
Sojourner Truth   II6
Trung Trac and Trung Nhi   I20

was very excited when I was first asked to write the foreword for this book. Lilith Fair is one of the most meaningful and joyous events to occur in my life and it's something I'm very proud to be a part of. In being the spokesperson for Lilith, I've learned so much — not only about myself but about the ever-changing and evolving attitudes towards women in our society. I've seen first-hand both the prejudice against and the adulation for this supposedly daring act. People say I had a lot of courage to put something like this together, but I simply felt that it was something that needed to be done, and luckily, I had the resources to help make it happen.

Courage. . . There are so many women who, due to their circumstances, have to muster all their courage just to face each day. They do this out of the spotlight and for no other reason than that they believe in what they're doing. They are the single mothers; the students fighting for acceptance in university programs dominated by men; the women who fight prejudice every day on the job simply because they are women; the homemakers who choose to stay at home and raise their children instead of working outside the home. These everyday acts of courage are to be respected and admired. As well, we have to acknowledge all the women who paved the way before us — our mothers, and their mothers before them, who had a long hard battle to fight. They helped to shape our world, making it a much better place for women today. My own story is called courageous, yet I was just doing what felt right.

I grew up in a fairly traditional home with loving parents who did their best to give me all the tools I needed to survive. They saw from an early age that I was very interested in art and music and they gave me every opportunity to nurture these desires, with music lessons and Saturday morning art classes at the art college. This they encouraged only as a lovely hobby, however, and not something suitable to enter into as a profession. As I grew, so did my understanding of how much I didn't fit in, which made for an interesting and tumultuous adolescence. But music and art remained a safe haven throughout the storm – something I knew that I was good at, something that gave me strength.

When I was seventeen, I joined a band. During our first gig, Mark Jowett from Nettwerk Records heard me sing and approached me about working with his band, Moev. I, of course, was very excited but my parents said, absolutely *not*! In retrospect this was a good thing, as it allowed me to grow up a bit and hold out for something better. Nettwerk came back two years later and offered me a five record contract as a solo artist!

Although it was hard to tell my parents, knowing their disapproval, the opportunity meant too much for me to give up. This was my dream being offered to me on a silver platter and I just couldn't turn it down. It's funny – I didn't see it then, but now I realize that it was very a courageous step for me to take. I gave up my safe, boring life and moved 4,000 miles away from my family and friends to start fresh in Vancouver. Back then, I had little fear.

I had a relatively easy time settling in to my new life. I signed to a small independent label who, from the get-go, gave me 100% creative control over every aspect of my career. They opened up a whole new world for me and set me loose in it; a freedom I now realize is almost unheard of in this industry. And fortunately, I was able to work with very talented people who taught me so much and always respected my opinions.

As my career grew, so did my knowledge of the inner workings of the industry. I began to see a different set of rules being applied to women than those that existed for men. In radio, programmers often said, "we can't play two women back to back." The same attitudes prevailed four years ago when I wanted Paula Cole to open up for me on tour; certain promoters insisted, "You can't put two women on the same bill – people won't come!"

The summer festivals out there were completely male dominated even though there was a wealth of great and diverse music being made by women. This made no sense to me — why were we all lumped into one category of women's music? Why weren't we all regarded as unique and talented human beings? My reasons for Lilith were not wholly a reaction, yet these realities were part of the path towards its inception.

Ideas don't form in a vacuum. There are many elements that go into that elusive and mysterious thing called inspiration. The fact that there have been women's festivals happening all over North America for years, even though my knowledge of them was sadly limited, helped to create a space where my idea could be heard, accepted and brought into the mainstream.

While trying to come up with a name for the festival, I talked to people about women throughout history who had made a mark. And it was my dear friend Buffy, the writer of this book, who offered up Lilith as a possibility. The story of Lilith, as it turns out, is quite obscure and it took a bit of piecing together of all the versions to come up with a fairly cohesive one that reads something like this...

So it goes that Adam was created in God's likeness, and given Eden to do with what he would. God also made all the animals to keep Adam company. Adam saw the relationships the animals had with each other and wanted that for himself. He tried with the animals, but it wasn't enough, so he asked God to send him a mate, a partner like the other creatures had. God obliged by making Lilith and sending her to Adam. At first he was pleased, but then she opened her mouth, showing that she had a mind of her own. He wanted her to lie beneath him and she promptly refused, saying that they were equal and she would not be subservient to him. Adam flew into a tantrum, so Lilith took off to calmer territory. Adam cried to God to have her returned to him, so God sent three angels to find her; but Lilith would have no part of it. Since the story goes that Lilith was birthing hundreds of the devil's spawn daily, the angels warned her that if she didn't return, God would kill one hundred of her children a day (not very PC of him – funny how God never got a bad rap about that …) Despite the dire consequences, Lilith never went back to a subservient life with Adam.

Like any myth or religion, we take those parts that can guide us in our lives and discard those elements that displease us. The story of Lilith is no different. While she goes on to be vilified and called a demon, I choose to ignore this part of the story as it is surely only the rantings of terrified men who were trying to keep other women from getting any silly ideas. What is important is that Lilith made a difficult and courageous decision and, in doing so, fell out of favour with the men in her life. So it can be said that Lilith was perhaps the world's first feminist!

Lilith Fair has been praised as being a turning point for women in music. I prefer to think of it as an ongoing progression. While women are being featured on the stage and playlisted on radio stations like never before, women in North America still earn, on average, anywhere from 58 to 75 cents for every dollar a man earns. Some cite lack of positive role models for young women as the reason. This is not because women haven't done anything noteworthy but because our history books are written by men who write about their own history.

In this book you will read about several important historical women. Each of them has done something meaningful, yet our knowledge of them has been extremely limited. You'll also read about the women who participated in Lilith Fair – from the performers to the multimedia team – women who themselves are becoming role models for the next generation.

So, Lilith Fair was created for many reasons: the joy of sharing live music; the connection of like minds; the desire to create a sense of community that I felt was lacking in our industry... I did this with innocence, I did this with the desire to make things better. I think music has that gift: to give hope, to bring people to an elevated state of mind, to connect. I did this with the guidance and the boundless creative and business genius of my partners, Terry McBride, Dan Fraser, and Marty Diamond; three strong and wonderful men all happy to support and respect the ideas of a woman — me.

I hope the stories in this book help to give you the courage to pursue your goals, whatever they might be and despite what others might say. We are not alone. Beside every successful woman is a group of supportive friends and respectful colleagues. Our belief in one another is what unites us and encourages us to be our best. I truly believe that as women we have a rich and enduring past, an exciting present and a very hopeful future!

Peace and Love,
Sarah McLachlan

I'd like to thank Buffy for writing this book, the band and all the crew who have worked so hard, John and Cathryn, everyone at Nettwerk Records and Arista Records. To all the artists who appeared on Lilith Fair and to all the music lovers out there... thank you.

In the summer of 1997, Sarah McLachlan launched the inaugural Lilith Fair – a seven-week musical festival that would tour North America celebrating women in music. It was quite unlike anything I'd ever seen before.

I remember only vaguely the first rock concert I ever attended. It was a tragic affair characterized by garish lighting, terrible lyrics and a deluge of unnatural, pastel fabrics. While I don't even recall who I saw or even what kind of music they played, what I do remember is the feeling – the vibe– if I can borrow a term from the 60s.

It's often a feeling rather than a concrete memory that marks an event, whether it's a personal occasion like a birthday party or a huge, organized, commercial event like a concert. It's the feeling that lingers on, a feeling made of fragments and petal thin recollections.

I left the Lilith Fair show in a very different frame of mind from the one I was in when I arrived. I'd heard so much about the tour that I was suspicious it could live up to the hype. When words like "community" and "celebration" are bandied about so readily, it's often easy to expect empty commercialism or naive sentimentalism.

Introduction

Still, I went through the gates like everyone else, sported a Bioré nose strip for altogether too long and spent much of the afternoon struggling with a heavy burden of irony, a tsunami of cynicism and a moat of critical distance. I am, after all, a twenty-something writer.

But after a few hours of listening to music, wandering through the crowd, and eavesdropping, I succumbed to the vibe of Lilith. There was something there that couldn't be summed up by reviews or dismissed by those unwilling to let it in. When the crowd joined in to help the women of Lilith sing "Closer to Fine" with the Indigo Girls, all the distance created by rock venues and star systems became a dim memory. I actually felt like I was a part of what was happening on the stage and in the crowd. People throughout the stadium exchanged genuine smiles with one another. In the 90s we're apt to describe these moments in such glib, hip terms that a genuine flutter of joy in our stomachs is dismissed as just something we ate. But in so doing, we cheat ourselves.

These observations lead me to this book, a series of snapshots of Lilith Fair. It's a narrative of the tour's context, progression and future, a series of profiles of performers, and introductions to sixteen significant women from history.

I chose to include these historical women because I didn't know about any of them when I was a girl. Sadly, my gender suffers from a terrible ignorance of our past. Because the achievements of women are often left out of history books, young girls grow up without knowing that there's a long and proud lineage of women. We stumble into womanhood unaware of the successes of those who were once girls just like us. Including these women isn't simply about introducing role models, it's about sharing knowledge and paying homage.

I love the fact that young girls went to Lilith Fair and were slack-jawed in amazement when Fiona Apple channelled demons or when Mudgirl laid down a brutal riff. I love imagining that the same girls went home and started saving up for guitars or began writing lyrics. From the success of the female performers who toured with Lilith Fair to the women profiled in this book, we, the so-called fairer sex, should be aware of our heritage. It's great when we're impressed by the achievements of contemporary women, but we're also obliged to honour the women who came before us. Had the suffragettes not struggled for the right for women to vote, then there would be no Lilith Fair today — it's really that simple.

Of course, to fully document Lilith Fair would take a book this size devoted to each performer. And those of you looking for information on Tracy Chapman will be disappointed. Tracy is very concerned with privacy and the propagation of her image, and asked not to be interviewed or filmed during her Lilith dates. Since this tour was and is about community, respecting the wishes of performers is an absolute must.

Like many people who passed through the gates of Lilith Fair, I am grateful the tour came together, that I witnessed its success and that it's continuing for at least another year. On a very personal note, I'm delighted to contribute to an event that has spawned so much good. *From Lilith to Lilith Fair* is a document of this important tour, one written from my perspective as an audience member, a writer and a woman. And as I type these words I hope that I can share with you what Lilith Fair and the experience of writing this book have given to me... something very different from what I had when I first walked through the turnstiles.

The summer heat has risen and the clouds have pulled back to reveal a gleaming, metallic sky. The crowd is growing restless. Beads of perspiration form on smooth brows, hands push back silken locks, a mother's ever-watchful eye turns to her child clutching at her knee... the faint murmur of excitement is growing almost palpable. Names slip from mouth to ear to mouth and on through the crowds of fans.

But there is no menace here, no fear of violence or concern that someone might be crushed in a rush for the stage. Instead, there's a kind of gentle pulse, like the throb of a racing heartbeat on the inside of a wrist. The murmurs and whispers slowly build until there are words spilling out from the throng. All eyes are focused on the microphone and guitar waiting patiently at centre stage. Then there's a rustle of motion in the wings, and figures appear and begin to pluck out single notes from the shadows. Moments later, a woman strides out to the guitar, hoists its strap around her shoulder, beams to the audience and shouts out, "Welcome to Lilith Fair!"

Prologue

In the beginning there was rhythm – the most primal component of human life, the thing that measures and paces each breath. There is the pounding of waves on a shore, the flap of a bird's wings, the phases of the moon and, lastly, there's the pulse of the heart, a beat that marks the passage of our lives. It measures each second, minute, day, and year that we're on this stage, every one of us linked to the next by the rhythm of life.

With rhythm as the thread that binds the fabric of our lives together, it's no surprise that music is practically as old as the pulsing of blood in our veins. Before there was language, prehistoric mothers probably hummed soft melodies while rhythmically rocking their infants to sleep. Perhaps the old saying that music is the universal language is a cliché because it has resonance, because it is the truth.

Thus, in the beginning there was rhythm. And buried in the rhythm was the promise of a song. Despite the organic origins of rhythm, the story of song has its roots in the fertile loam of religion. Even though it's been a long time since music was simply in the realm of the divine, many musicians and fans alike would argue that it still retains its divine nature. Like prayer or confession, the power of music is in its wordless, intuitive fusion between the self and something greater.

Fans line the hills at The Gorge, George, Washington.

The secular practice of music is the norm now. The airwaves pulse with it and pop CDs are everywhere, from briefcases to backpacks. But even critics of music's fallen state can't deny that it can provide an ecstatic experience, with the live performance forming a holy covenant between performer and audience.

Surely anyone who's been to a concert will agree that a live performance yields something more powerful than just notes woven together by sound engineers and machinery. We all know this to be true, but why is it so? Perhaps it's the challenge — can the sound hold up without the smoke and mirrors of a recording studio? Maybe it's the intimacy, when the space between the music, audience and performers dissolves and creates a new product from all the disparate elements. Or maybe it's just cool to see the people behind the sounds we love. Whatever it is, live performances are all about pleasure. And if you blend a bunch of live performances together and call it a festival? It's a recipe for bliss.

North Americans love this formula. Give us some cold drinks, hot acts and a cool breeze and we'll be smiling till Labour Day. Accordingly, the music festival has an illustrious past in this part of the world. While music festivals have been happening all over the world since ancient times, the template for what we now identify as a rock music festival is probably the International Monterey Pop Festival.

It was an exciting time in music and culture when Monterey Pop took to the stage in June of 1967. This was the infamous summer of love, when an entire generation was invited to tune in, turn on and drop out. Unlike a typical rock concert, in which the show lasts a single day, Monterey Pop spanned three days and generated over twenty-five solid hours of music. But the festival isn't remembered solely for its timing and volume. Monterey Pop was both a musical zeitgeist and a launching pad. With a performance roster that included the Grateful Dead, Jefferson Airplane, Janis Joplin and Jimi Hendrix, Monterey was as much a cultural phenomenon as it was a musical event.

From the spirit of Monterey came the legendary Woodstock. A happy hippie pastoral event that anticipated an attendance of fewer than 200,000 and drew close to a million, Woodstock became an out-of-control symbol of 60s excess with free love, drugs and groovy vibes quickly becoming more important than the music slipping through the clouds of marijuana smoke. Some Woodstock goers claim to have witnessed breathtaking performances by Creedence Clearwater Revival,

Backstage with Lisa Loeb, Beth Orton, Sarah McLachlan, and Michelle Malone.

11

Vancouver, BC fans in the rain.

The Band, Jefferson Airplane and Santana, not to mention Jimi Hendrix's now mythical version of "The Star Spangled Banner," yet the conventional wisdom about Woodstock is that if you can remember it, you weren't really there.

There were a number of significant music festivals that followed the success of Monterey Pop and Woodstock. The Rolling Stones and a host of rock 'n' roll heroes gave a free concert at the Altamont Speedway that ended in disaster, with a stabbing death and a wave of criticism over how the event was mismanaged. Yet even with the dark spectre of Altamont hanging over the rock festival's head, the basic formula of the event thrived. People enjoyed seeing a wide range of performers on one bill, it was great for the box office, and performers liked being able to see each other play.

Since the late 60s there has been a deluge of rock festivals, from those spanning several days to huge stadium concerts that ran for fewer than twelve hours. Some of these multi-performer events were about the almighty dollar, but some were about charitable fund raising – like Bob Geldof's Live Aid. Others were simply about community.

Community is certainly a strong motivation behind the Michigan Womyn's Music Festival, a quarter-century old, exclusively female music and performance event. Michigan, and the over twenty other women-oriented festivals scattered around the US and Canada, are the older sisters of Lilith Fair. With a focus on lesbian politics, demands for female empowerment and a decidedly folk flavour, these women's music festivals aren't easily confused with mainstream rock fests. Michigan and the other female-oriented festivals have worked hard to carve out a niche in a world of music where stacked Marshall amps rule and the person twiddling the knobs is almost certainly a man.

Differences aside, the one common denominator to all these musical events is their fixed locations. Until the early 1990s most music festivals kept themselves firmly rooted in the earth: they were conceived in one city, they grew up there and it was there that they died.

But in the spring of 1991 Perry Farrell, then of the band Jane's Addiction, decided to take his music, both the kind that he made and the kind that he liked, on the road. Dubbed Lollapalooza, the tour featured contemporary acts like Nine Inch Nails and the Butthole Surfers, boasted an extensive mosh pit, spoken-word tents and even a village selling food, crafts and other merchandise. Lollapalooza uprooted the musical festival and transplanted it into patches of earth all over North America.

The B stage.

Meredith Brooks laughs with interviewer.

On the heels of Lollapalooza came travelling shows like HORDE, and, particularly in Canada, Another Roadside Attraction. But by 1996 the formula was looking just that: formulaic. Touring festivals became known for their aggressive fans, loud music, and the conspicuous absence of women on stage.

Admittedly, there has been some female presence: Hole and Sinéad O'Connor have both stepped up to the mike at Lollapalooza, Sheryl Crow has joined Another Roadside Attraction and Natalie Merchant has toured with HORDE, but for the most part, the role of women artists has been very limited.

So the question remains: where are the women? Certainly there are some in catering, some in the ticket booths and plenty in the crowd, but why the hell aren't they on the stage? At first glance the absence of women from such visible and commercially successful events seems something of an anomaly. For, while the stages of Lollapalooza and HORDE were dominated by men, the pop charts were swelling with women – from the smooth tones of Erykah Badu to the anthemic assertions of Meredith Brooks.

With this kind of exclusion being standard fare in the music business, many female artists chafed at a male-dominated industry that benefitted from their labours but denied them their rewards. Out of that frustration, and also prompted by a sense of responsibility, women began to band together to create CDs and concerts that benefitted others. At the same time, they gave themselves the gift of camaraderie. But while these actions and events began to happen in isolation, a night here and a release there, there were few solid forums for female voices.

This exclusion remains a mystery. Women are more visible in the music industry now than ever before. From Madonna's chart busting pop rhythms and everyone's favourite alterna-freak Björk, to the eviscerating cries of Ms. Polly Jean Harvey, "the ladies," to quote Queen Latifah, "are first."

Rolling Stone, in its recent "Women in Rock" edition, published a list of all the years that have been heralded as "The Year of Women in Rock." It was an ironic inclusion: the list itself took up more space than some music magazines will devote to female artists in a given issue.

Clearly, the success of women in music cannot be ignored, but that doesn't mean it isn't patronized. Even with the ladies pushing into the locker rooms of music, there's still something odd about the way the press handles the coverage. All too often the press will relegate the work of radically different artists – say art popster Suzanne Vega and riot grrrls L7 – to a generic category like "women's music" and cast it to the sidelines. Sadly, this kind

Profile

Artemisia Gentileschi
1593–1652/3

When Artemisia Gentileschi was born in Italy in the 16th century, teaching a woman to read and write was unusual, and teaching her the language of pigments and hues was out of the question. Yet Artemisia's father, Orazio, a follower of Caravaggio, made certain his daughter knew her way around a palette.

With a blank canvas in front of her, Artemisia was able to shake off the pall of the repressive times she was born into. Her first dated painting, *Susanna and the Elders*, was infused with her obvious knowledge of colour and anatomy, but perhaps more significantly, the painting showed a female heroine – an uncommon choice for that period of time.

In 1612 Artemisia was raped by one of her instructors, Agostino Tassi. The matter was brought to court where both the accused and Artemisia were thoroughly questioned. To determine whether Artemisia was telling the truth, she was subjected to a 17th century version of a lie detector test. Metal rings were fastened to her fingers and slowly tightened during her interrogation. Due to the extreme pain involved, it often caused people to confess to crimes even if they were innocent. Despite the painful questioning, Artemisia's testimony remained unchanged. Even so, Tassi served less than a year in prison.

In the aftermath of the trial Artemisia, her reputation in tatters, went back to painting. By the age of 23 she had become a well-known artist within Italy. But the battles of sexism continued. Her work commanded a much lower price than work by her male peers, and many critics were quick to reduce her to being a mere imitator of Caravaggio.

Yet Artemisia never doubted herself, daring detractors to compare her work to that of her contemporaries. Thankfully, modern critics have begun to recognize her work and now, almost 350 years after her death, it is finally receiving the consideration it deserves.

of ignorance is nothing new. It's a common enough practice to identify the large and diverse contribution women make to the music industry as women's music, simply for ease of identification.

One result of this superficial grouping is that women are often placed in unnatural competition with one another. Ask a contemporary female performer about getting radio airplay and you'll hear the same story. "I can't put you into the rotation this week," says the DJ in Anytown. "I've already added Alanis, Tori, Sarah or *anyotherwoman*, so I can't add another." The assumption behind this absurd argument is that women all occupy the same space in music, so why would you need two?

This flawed logic doesn't end there. Not only does it restrict the number of women getting on radio playlists, but it's also why concert promoters feel that two women on the same touring bill is strictly *verboten*. Case in point: the now legendary tale of Sarah McLachlan and Paula Cole.

Part way through her *Fumbling Towards Ecstasy* tour, Sarah thought it would be great to have Paula, another multi-talented performer, added to the bill as an opening act. That, however, was easier thought than done. "Two women?" scoffed promoters, "Forget it. It'll never work." Sarah angrily pushed for

Sarah and Paula perform "Big Yellow Taxi."

18

an explanation. "Nobody wants to pay to see two women in one night," they declared. And the reason? "Well," they blustered, "because that's the way it is."

Rather than letting go of her anger or simply forgetting about the whole idea, Sarah pushed to get what she wanted and did end up touring with Paula. But what the promoters said left its mark – though not in a way that they might have anticipated. As she tried to understand where they were coming from and why they'd tried their best to dissuade her, she realized more and more that she simply didn't believe what the promoters told her.

Sarah, who has been in the business since her late teens, began meditating about the absence of women from musical events, despite their formidable position on the music charts. Slowly the threads of an idea wound through the young singer-songwriter's head. "What about an all-female tour?" she mused.

The idea slowly took form and expanded as she discussed it with friends and business partners. But it was still quite some time before what Sarah first called "Girliepalooza" became more than an idle fantasy.

Cassandra Wilson and band play basketball backstage.

nd here the story of Lilith Fair truly begins, although a long while passed between its conception and its birth. Unlike the goddess Athena springing from the head of Zeus, Lilith Fair did not leap fully formed from the dreams of Sarah McLachlan.

While Sarah was contemplating women's inequality in the music business, she was actually supposed to be writing a new album. In fact, her original plan was to retreat to a chalet in the mountains of Quebec, far from the travails of the music industry, and emerge, rejuvenated, with a beautiful new album in hand.

But the songs were reluctant to appear, and just fragments and whispers darted across her notebook and through her recording sessions. When it became clear that Sarah wasn't in the right spirit to dive into the album, her manager, Terry McBride, opted for some dynamic motivation, suggesting that maybe she should go out and do some live shows. "I thought it would get her into a musical headspace," he recalled. Sarah was uncertain at first, having just left the narrow confines of her tour bus, but finally agreed, as long as she wouldn't be asked to headline.

Easy enough. Sarah opened for Sting on two Canadian dates and agreed to do a mini-fest to help her lure the muse, and her music, back. Her one condition? Only women performers. The shows were a tremendous success and, by the fourth show in Vancouver, had begun to take on a life of their own. In response, Sarah gave them a name: Lilith Fair.

"We came into things too late in the season to put on a whole tour," Sarah remembers. "And it would have simply taken too much time out of my writing." So these first four shows served as training runs for Sarah and the other members of the Lilith team: her managers, Dan Fraser and Terry McBride, and her agent Marty Diamond. "We had to figure out how many people we needed to run it, how we would organize it and, honestly, to see if it would work," she explains.

These shows did more than work – they sold out. Hardly surprising, given the talent involved. The mini-tour had an impressive lineup, boasting the likes of Patti Smith, Aimee Mann, Suzanne Vega, Lisa Loeb and Sarah herself.

This brief excursion into a world of musical women convinced Sarah that an all-woman tour would be good for the public and the artists alike.

"The idea of creating some kind of camaraderie that didn't exist before was so important to me," she says. "Because the music industry pits us against each other, it's vital that we're able to bring a group of women together so that we can support each other, so that we can learn from each other."

Getting her agent and management team to support the idea of an all-woman tour was the easy part. The difficulty lay in convincing the promoters, media and audiences, as well as assembling a roster that would live up to what the team envisioned. "We were an unknown quantity," Sarah admits. "No one knew what they were getting into."

Even with no track record in festival organization, the Lilith organizers were bold in their pursuit of stellar talent. "We all thought about what we wanted from a tour," says Sarah, "and then came back to the table with a wish list of performers we wanted to have."

Had the group had radically differing musical tastes, the story of Lilith Fair might never have happened. As it was, when the four came together to compare their wish lists, they discovered they had written down many of the same names.

Most names that were discussed in the beginning did appear on the posters for Lilith 1997, with a few exceptions. "We wanted Neneh Cherry, we wanted Erykah Badu, we wanted Liz Phair, but we didn't get them," laments McBride. "Some of the women we wanted were touring; some were recording. But I think we'll get them next year," he adds hopefully.

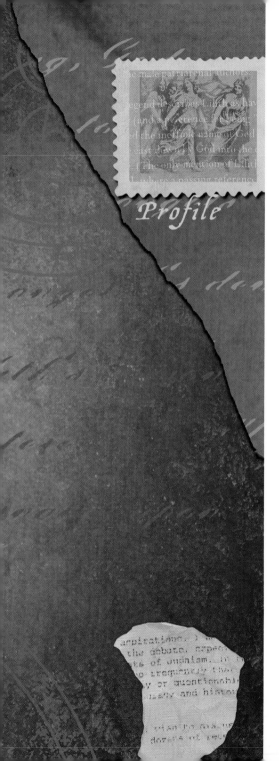

Countess Ada Lovelace

1815–1852

❧ **While much has been written** about about the the scandals of the notorious Lord Byron, much could also be written about the achievements of his daughter Ada Lovelace – the world's first computer programmer.

Only five weeks after Ada's birth to Lord and Lady Byron, Ada's mother demanded a separation from the notorious poet and the pair split, with sole custody awarded to the mother. Fearing that her child would adopt the debauched lifestyle of her father, Lady Byron steered her daughter towards science and mathematics, although it is said that Ada, who inherited the poetic inclinations of her father, argued instead for a "poetical science."

Ada's aptitude for the sciences blossomed after her first encounter with the work of computing pioneer Charles Babbage. At a dinner party held by a friend, she heard about his idea for a calculating machine called an Analytical Engine. Inspired, Ada decided to send Babbage a translation she had done from a French article on a lecture Babbage had delivered in Italy. Babbage was so impressed with her work that he encouraged her to add her own notes, which she enthusiastically did: the notes ended up being longer than the original article.

The two exchanged many letters over the years, and eventually Ada suggested to Babbage that his machine might also be used to create graphics, compose music, and serve a wide range of purposes beyond those of the scientific community. She also sent him a proposal for how the analytical engine could be used to produce Bernoulli numbers – the first computer program. In 1979, a software language developed by the US Department of Defense was named "Ada" in her honour.

In a world where girls are still pushed away from science and even their dolls hate math, a 19th century computer geek in a corset is definitely something to celebrate.

Village stage musician Kinnie Starr.

After the main lineup had been determined, the organizers soon realized that with such amazing female talent clamouring to be heard, a second stage was a must-have. And when the line-up for that stage was filled?

"We just didn't have the heart to keep saying no to these performers," says McBride, "so we created the Village stage to open up another twenty slots." The addition of the Village stage captured the spirit of Lilith, a spirit that longs to give everyone a chance.

"For us," says Sarah, "both the B stage and the Village stage are really important because that's where you get a lot of young artists who usually don't have the opportunity to play in front of such a huge group. When you're doing the bar circuit," she explains, "you may be playing to an audience of only a few hundred people at best." But the B stage lets the artists shine in front of thousands. "It's a fantastic feeling to find these performers who are just starting out and give them the opportunity to have these bigger audiences and to have the media attention they might not otherwise get."

As the group began to recruit performers, the buzz around the tour also grew. At first it was from people in the music business, wondering how they could get involved, but soon, corporate America came knocking on Lilith's door.

Very quickly it seemed like everyone wanted to slap their trademarks on Lilith. Tour organizers however, weren't listening… at least at first. In the beginning the team agreed that they didn't really need the money, that corporate sponsorship wasn't really what they were about. But they reconsidered when it became apparent that companies were willing to donate to charities of Lilith's choice.

With charitable fundraising as their main goal, Lilith Fair created four categories for sponsors: Learning, Wellness, Spirit and Shelter. But it took more than money to become a sponsor of Lilith Fair. The tour actually left the Spirit and Wellness categories open because no one who had expressed interest lived up to the requirements. The team also turned down companies on the grounds that they weren't clean. "Socially conscious business is what we wanted," Sarah told the *Wall Street Journal*. "No child labour, no animal testing." The money from the sponsors was then donated to one of several charities. Borders donated a portion of the proceeds from on-site record sales to Lifebeat, a music industry AIDS organization, and RAINN, the Rape, Abuse & Incest National Network, founded by Tori Amos. Nine West and Lilith Fair both donated to the the Strang Cornell Breast Center of New York, and Bioré donated

Juliana Hatfield and Betty.

27

Profile

E. Pauline Johnson (Tekahionwake)
1861 – 1913

In this era of cultural fusion, a woman of mixed racial background isn't considered unusual. But in the 1800s, being a "half breed" was often a curse that kept an individual trapped between worlds, unwelcome in both.

For many mixed-race people the goal was to "pass." Those with light skin would often deny their heritage and call themselves white. Writer and poet E. Pauline Johnson could pass, but she refused to try.

Born in 1861 on the Six Nations reserve in Ontario, Johnson was the daughter of a Mohawk chief and a white woman. She grew up on the reserve but was kept separate from the other Mohawk children. This created differences that were apparent both in her physical appearance and in the way she experienced the world.

It was exactly those differences that she showcased when she performed her poetry. She divided her recitals into two sections. The first half was performed in a shimmering ball gown, the second in full Indian garb – bear claws and all.

Choosing to call herself by her grandfather's name, Tekahionwake, which means "double life" in the Mohawk language, Johnson stated, "my aim, my joy, my pride is to sing the glories of my own people." Much of her work revolved around the native legends she'd been told in her childhood. While white authors tended to represent natives as a tragic, vanishing culture, Johnson strove to remind people that these cultures were still vibrant, even in a world that seemed intent on their destruction.

While some contemporary critics have dismissed her work as too romantic and inaccurate, her legacy continues. Tekahionwake is widely regarded as the earliest Canadian native writer to explore native topics in fiction and poetry, and is lauded as both an entertainer and a rebel.

$20,000 each to all the charities, which also included IRSA, the International Rett Syndrome Association; WOW, Wider Opportunities for Women; and ANAD, the National Association of Anorexia Nervosa and Associated Disorders.

This didn't seem enough for Sarah, who believed she could both push the envelope and fill it with cash. "I feel a responsibility as a human being to give something back. I am in a position of power, where we are making a lot of money on this tour," she says. In her eyes, it's not about being noble. "When we pull out in our tour buses, we should be leaving behind something other than torn-up lawns and litter." And indeed they did: one dollar from every ticket sold went to local charities, 85% of which were domestic violence centres.

Picking out which charities to donate money to was definitely more difficult than raising the cash. Donna Westmoreland, concourse manager for 1997 and director of marketing for 1998, spent considerable time researching the charities. "We asked local promoters to give us names, and then began investigating each name we got," says Westmoreland. She was looking for efficient organizations that worked closely with the communities they served. "So if they had absurdly high administrative costs in their annual report, we didn't go with

Sarah at The Gorge.

them," she explains. "But honestly, I didn't come across anyone who wasn't worthy. It was very difficult to tell someone why they weren't getting the money."

Westmoreland then sought out vendors for the Village. "I think we are the first tour to try to make sure our vendors are socially responsible. We said they had to make the jewelry and clothes themselves, or know about the conditions in which their products were made."

So with performers, sponsors, charities, vendors and venues in place, Lilith, which had learned to crawl the year before, was poised to take its first steps.

After months of planning, the first Lilith Fair tour began on a beautiful day at The Gorge, a natural amphitheatre in George, Washington. Even though the excitement levels around the event had been climbing steadily for months, there was no lightning bolt when the first notes rang out. Nor was there a thunderous kick-off to the ground-breaking event.

Instead, the festival's inaugural moments took place on the Village stage. Sarah McLachlan, barefoot and smiling, climbed the low platform, picked up her guitar and began to sing – an unassuming beginning to what became the most successful tour of the summer.

Kim Fox faces the press.

Sarah McLachlan opens Lilith Fair 1997 at The Gorge near George, Washington.

Even the tour's first press conference was without pretense. Sarah spent her time with the media squinting into the sun rather than putting on sunglasses, simply because she didn't want to look like a rock star. Oddly, there was an uncomfortable feeling to the conference, though it's hard to say whether the unease came from the performers or the press. But there was definitely something amiss. Perhaps it's because no one knew what questions to ask, or they were hesitant to ask the obvious ones about shared cycles or lipstick.

Yet, as the day progressed, the uneasy spirit troubling the press conference fled, perhaps chased away by the watchful spirit of Lilith. Whatever prompted the mood shift, by the time the main stage began pulsing with the sounds of Suzanne Vega, Jewel, and Paula Cole, and the B and Village stages began rocking to Mudgirl, Lauren Hoffman, Leah Andreone and Kinnie Starr, it didn't matter. The girls rocked the house and the sold-out crowd of 20,000 was right there with them.

As the first show drew to a close, after a day of cheering and singing left everyone exhausted but happy, it was clear that Lilith had finally returned to the garden of Eden, triumphant and unbowed.

The next three shows, in Salem, Oregon, and Mountain View and Irvine, California were all sold out, bringing Lilith's ticket sales to just under 70,000 in only four days. The women were all delighted, but hardly surprised. As Sarah remarks, "I would have been disappointed in humanity had the shows not done well."

While the event was being touted as simply a "celebration of women in music," everyone knew it wouldn't be perceived as that. Early on, the press conferences became lightning rods for gender issues, with Sarah often bearing the brunt of the questions. But, over time, there was a shift in the way these questions were fielded. While Sarah, as the driving force behind the tour, was expected to trumpet, defend and wax poetic about Lilith in each city and every interview, it's clear that the other artists involved were beginning to feel protective about both the tour and each other.

When a reporter suggested that the tour wasn't diverse enough, Kinnie Star jumped in with her own views on the matter. "It's Sarah's show," she said, "and it's up to her to pick music she likes." And then, to everyone's surprise, she announced that she was planning her own three-girl tour with Veda Hille and Oh Susanna. With moments like these, the community Sarah longed

Suzanne Vega and Kinnie Starr.

33

for began to take shape. It seemed that everyone was beginning to really support one another, whether it be with a spare guitar pick or a shoulder to lean on.

Kim Bingham, aka Mudgirl, one of the artists who helped launch the tour, seemed happy to be in the company of women. "We definitely need to make a concerted effort to promote the work of women in the music industry, because it is male dominated. Most of us who work in this business know that, and have learned the hard way, from playing multiple bills where there is only one female-fronted act in the entire fest." Before the tour began Kim was both curious and excited. "It was very important for me to get on the bill because I'm a woman and I wanted to share this experience with all these other female performers. I think there's a connection between this happening," she laughs, "and the Pathfinder landing on Mars."

Sometimes, the Fair did look like it was on another planet, perhaps Venus. When Rasputina, a chamber-pop trio, did a warm-up session in the parking lot, the scene was magical, and nothing like what you'd expect to see at a summer music festival: three women with cellos bowing away amid tour vans, diesel exhaust and a rushing crew.

For many of the performers on the tour, that was part of what Lilith was about: allowing performers the freedom to do the

Rasputina

unexpected, to do what they wanted. From Jewel's yodelling to Paula Cole's spartan vocal performance on the acoustic stage there was a comfortable, leisurely pace that encouraged performers to do what they felt like doing.

The tour also gave Lisa Loeb the rare opportunity to do a pared down solo performance. Even though she often plays with a band, performing alone with just a guitar is still a real pleasure. "A lot of people know me from just one song that was on the radio. One or two songs," she insists, "isn't enough to really understand what it is that I do. It has been really nice just getting up as a musician, not as a pop singer."

Lisa Loeb.

Tracy Bonham joined the show mid-July and immediately started rocking the house with plenty of power-sawing on her souped-up violin. With painted flames racing up the fiddle's face, it's no surprise that the instrument, and the woman who wields it, created such a stir.

For Tracy, though, there was much more to this tour than crowds and applause. Being in the company of women was something she needed, even if she wasn't aware of it until after she toured with seven guys for nine months. "I thought I could do it, and I did, but I really missed having female companionship. At first I didn't think it was necessary. But I'm just starting to realize that it's important to have someone you can really connect with."

Moon
Mercury
Venus
Sun
Mars
Jupiter
Saturn
ed Stars
e mover

Profile

Elizabeth Cady Stanton
1815 – 1902

❧ **Some people think political activity,** especially voting, is a waste of time. "Nothing ever changes," they explain, "so why bother?" Yet if you consider Elizabeth Cady Stanton's lifelong battle for suffrage, voting doesn't seem like much trouble after all.

Stanton was born to a well-heeled family in New York state, when having two X chromosomes was a cross to bear. She knew early on that her parents wished she were a boy – her father often shared his disappointment with the young Elizabeth.

But she was undeterred, and Stanton matched and bettered her brothers' every achievement. Still, she knew it was a man's world. This became painfully clear when she and her husband travelled to an international abolitionist conference in London, England.

Stanton's education, conviction and determination meant nothing there. A woman, they told her, could not be an official delegate. Enraged, Stanton, and another woman who was not allowed to participate, planned to hold a women's rights conference when back in the US.

Eight years later they made good on their promise. On July 19, 1848, in Seneca Falls, NY, a group of women met to discuss women's rights. Stanton was the intellectual force behind the group and it was there that she delivered The Seneca Falls Declaration of Sentiments. The document included a bill of rights and a long list of demands for female equality, including the right to vote.

Stanton began working with fellow suffragette Susan B. Anthony, and the pair's lifelong friendship built a movement that eventually did win the vote for women. Unfortunately, neither woman lived long enough to witness their own victory. But they left a proud legacy: on August 26, 1920, the final passage of the Suffrage Amendment passed in Congress and American women finally had the right to vote.

Sarah McLachlan and Emily Saliers
perform "Water is Wide."

And the connections are made everywhere at Lilith Fair: between the sets, behind dressing room doors, over meals and even centre stage. According to Sarah, it was the arrival of the Indigo Girls, Amy Ray and Emily Saliers, that really kicked in the tour's growing sense of community and many collaborations. "They just started knocking on dressing room doors and suddenly everyone was hanging out."

If the old theories about women on the road had any truth to them, then this is the point where the cat fights would begin – with snide remarks being whispered behind unsuspecting backs as the Lilith girls splintered off into high school-like cliques. But this just never happened.

As much fun as the stage performances were, the real magic was created in Sarah's dressing room, when the artists all practised together, cramming to learn some of each others' songs in time for the show. The images of the rehearsal are as potent as the songs: there's Sarah, lightheartedly conducting the other singers with one hand in the air, Amy and Emily leaning forward to sing the song's title line, Jewel bobbing forward emphatically as she sings. When someone misses a cue warm laughter rings out, while a lounging dog looks around in confusion.

For the thousands of fans who didn't have access to the sleep-over camp vibe backstage, the bonding became clear a little later on — in the form of collaborations on stage. This is what Sarah had longed for, the fusion of creative talents into one dynamic, supportive environment. While there had been a handful of artists gracing other performer's stages before this point, such collaborations soon became the norm, and the women visibly grew very comfortable with each other.

The Indigo Girls (Amy Ray and Emily Saliers) with Shawn Colvin.

"Everybody is here not only to enjoy their own shows and enjoy performing for such a great crowd, but most of all to experience everybody else's music," says Emily. When the Indigo Girls invited all the other performers to join them for songs, it was sometimes a little overwhelming. "I can barely sing when I look over and see the women who are sharing the stage with us," she added. "It's very moving to me."

Perhaps the most significant of the collaborations, besides the Indigo Girls' "Closer to Fine," was the song that ended both Sarah's set and the event — Joni Mitchell's "Big Yellow Taxi." Why this song? Joni Mitchell was a performer most of these musicians grew up on, a woman in the boys' club way before the idea of "women in music" became a marketing dream.

Profile

Emma Goldman
1869 – 1940

Avenging angel to some, and red devil to others, many things have been said about Emma Goldman. She's been lauded as a feminist and a writer, branded a madwoman, and was even described as a "moral pervert" by Teddy Roosevelt.

Regardless of what Goldman was, she began life like everyone else – yelling. Emma, however, chose not to stop. Born in Kovo, Lithuania, Emma was forced to emigrate to America at the age of fifteen after refusing to marry a man her father had chosen for her.

It was in Chicago that Emma became enthralled by the labour and anarchist movements. After the Haymarket Square tragedy in 1886, where a bomb was thrown into a crowd of police during a workers' demonstration, four anarchists were hanged – not because they threw the bomb, but because they were anarchists. This incident led her to decide to become a revolutionary.

Goldman moved to New York and joined the Yiddish Anarchist movement. She is often called the mother of anarchy in America, but she was also its doctor, teacher, lover and comrade, for she fought political battles on almost every front. As publisher of the radical periodical *Mother Earth*, she attacked the repressive, classist regimes of her day, and advocated birth control and suffrage. "True emancipation," said Goldman, "begins neither at the polls nor in courts. It begins in women's souls." Goldman was repeatedly jailed for a number of reasons, from inciting riots to opposing World War I to advocating birth control. "Keep your minds open," Emma warned women, "and your wombs closed."

Deported to Russia in 1919, her hopes for the Russian Revolution vanished because of the political persecution and forced labour she witnessed. She continued to write about this disillusionment throughout her life.

Goldman died in Toronto in 1940, but she was buried in Chicago not far from the Haymarket Martyrs whose fate had changed her life.

Joan Osborne wears a Planned Parenthood t-shirt onstage in Houston, Texas.

The bonds forged over the tour needed to bear the weight of ignorance in Houston, Texas, when the women of Lilith hit one of the tour's few snags. In addition to donating a portion of ticket sales to women's organizations, Lilith also used its village as an opportunity for women's groups to hand out information and brochures dealing with topics ranging from birth control to politics. Unfortunately, in Houston, they hit a wall when the venue management refused to let Planned Parenthood, a pro-choice organization, set up a booth.

"It seemed really hypocritical on their part," said Joan Osborne. "They were willing to have Lilith Fair in their venue, and were willing to make money off it, but not to support all the other things the Fair was about." Considering that the Fair's political acts were an important part of the tour for Joan, she was more than a little ticked off.

It was the eleventh hour, and no one knew what to do. All the tickets had been sold and cancelling the show in protest wouldn't do anything but break the hearts of thousands of fans — and cheat a local charity out of much needed money. The show must go on, the women decided. But they also tried to think of some way to fight back.

The press conference became the perfect place to protest. "We were told we had control of this," said Sarah, visibly angered. "We made everyone aware of the kind of stuff we would be doing. It's not like they didn't know what we were about."

The news of the battle reached the stadium's owner who hastily reversed his employee's earlier decision to bar the pro-choice group. "I think it was because Sarah and I said something at the press conference" said Joan. "Fortunately, we are in a position of power and were able to do something about it." In a tour that seemed to be characterized by an endless succession of triumphs, this was another moment when the Fair felt it was making a difference, one fan and one venue at a time.

Ah, but despite all those victories and the supportive trappings of Lilith's welcoming bosom, like the massage therapy, girlie gab sessions and shared boxes of Midol, a tour is still a tour. To produce such an event, everyone from crew to performer must leave the safety and comfort of home to live in what feels likes an endless succession of boxes: the box of the bus, the box of the hotel room, the box of the dressing room.

Beth Orton, a wickedly mischievous Brit, is quite candid about the horrors of living in a van. In the midst of a venue-wide rampage on a golf cart she had "nicked" when someone's head was turned, Beth stops to dish out the dirt. "This is a bit disgusting but," she confides, "no solids in the toilet, and that includes toilet

Beth Orton at the wheel of the "nicked" golf cart.

Peace, Love, and Credit Accepted in The Village.

paper." This is an essential tip that if forgotten, means hands must be plunged into rather unpleasant liquids. "Glamorous?" she snorts. "Yeah, really."

As far as being able to travel to interesting places? Well, not exactly. Last year, Tracy Bonham had the opportunity to tour Australia, a place she's always longed to visit. And did she get to throw boomerangs and cradle baby koala bears while she was touring down under? Well, not quite. "There was one picture in my camera from the trip," she sighs, "and it was of the hotel room." Lilith Fair was much the same, as concert venues are often situated well outside the bustle of the nearest city. And as for photo ops, well, hotel ceilings are pretty much the same, regardless of what town they happen to be in.

There are some compensations though. For Cassandra Wilson, the kinships forged on the road make up for all the nightmares of such an unusual lifestyle. "The best thing is the camaraderie, the jokes that you tell, the shared experiences," she says. "I always sing that Willie Nelson song 'On the Road Again' on the road. It's about bonding with people and making music." So would she say she's a fan of this way of life?

"Not exactly," she admits, her nose wrinkling. "The worst thing is people putting their shoes right next to your bunk!

I wake up in the middle of the night, reach outside of my bunk and there are two pairs of shoes and they're not mine. And when you're on the road with guys there is a certain flavour they have," Cassandra adds delicately. "I don't know what they call it," she says with a shrug. "But it's strong and pungent."

You'd think that for Roberta Carter Harrison of the Wild Strawberries, the tour might have been too much of a challenge, seeing as she was pregnant. But apparently not. Come next Lilith Fair, Roberta and her bandmate/husband Ken Harrison are just going to "put a little bassinet between the beds and keep rocking!"

Roberta was thrilled to be part of this sea-change event, both as a woman and as an up-and-coming chanteuse. On a professional level, she knew that appearing on the side stage would have her playing to much larger crowds than she had played to before. "We'd never have this kind of exposure in, for example, Minneapolis. We played there last year for about a hundred people and it's times how many zeros today?"

Michelle Malone agreed that the side stages were a blessing, and added that being there didn't diminish her experience at all. "I was really surprised that I didn't feel any less a part of the Fair," she commented. According to Michelle, being

Rock For Choice booth in The Village.

Jill Sobule and Joy Askew.

on what she called the "little baby stage" wasn't much different than singing on the main stage with the Indigo Girls.

In fact it was home to many talented artists, including marathon scrabble players Joy "scrabble keeps you sane" Askew and Jill "that is not a word" Sobule. "We made jokes about the eenie weenie stage," says Joy. "But at this stage in my career I need to get to know people – people don't know me. While I've played on these big stages with Joe Jackson or Laurie Anderson or Peter Gabriel, I've never had the intimacy of a small stage. And I love it!" she exclaims.

In fact, sometimes it was to the performers' disadvantage to appear on the main stage. One of the more unfortunate events at a Lilith show happened when Tibetan singer Yungchen Lhamo took to the stage in Montage Mountain, PA, opening her performance by dedicating it to His Holiness, the Dalai Lama. It was early and the venue was just beginning to fill up. According to a crew member, those present acted like they'd just discovered beer, and didn't know when to stop drinking. The unruly few continued to yell and hoot during her set and did a fair job of drowning out her efforts.

Luckily, this sad example of what Lilith is working against was an isolated one. Yungchen's other sets had the audience in enraptured silence – some even meditating in the midst of the crowd. Having grown up in a place were women's freedom is gravely restricted, Yungchen thinks that the Lilith performers and fans have much to celebrate. "I see so many women at this concert and I think they are so lucky," she says. "I hope that those young women understand what freedom means."

Many of the musicians on the bill had never met before and, after bathing in Lilith's warmth, were often reluctant to leave. "We're all really sad that we have to leave and go back to the real world," said Kelly Willis on her last day. "I had a lot of fun and got to hear a lot of great music and see a lot of great women do their jobs really well. It was very encouraging and inspiring."

"My assessment," said Sheryl Crow, "is that people feel as if they're a part of something that hasn't happened before." "There hasn't been one dodgy incident," adds Shawn Colvin, "not one. All of this has been done so professionally and is running on such good energy." Shawn, who stole Montreal's heart with her broken, amiable French, was thrilled to be able to hang out with all the women, a new experience for her despite the years she has been in the business, touring and recording.

Yungchen Lhamo interviewed before show in Pennsylvania.

47

Profile

Hannah Senesh
1921–44

Hannah Senesh was born in Hungary at a time when the world seemed against everything she was: a woman, a Jew, and a fiercely honourable individual. As Europe began its descent into the darkness preceding World War II, she watched her country of birth look less and less like home. When Jews' rights started disappearing, Senesh dreamed of Palestine and a Jewish homeland. On Rosh Hashana in 1939, she waved goodbye to her weeping mother and boarded a train to what she hoped was truly the promised land.

While there, thoughts of World War II weighed heavily on the young Zionist's heart. She longed to rescue her family, but it was impossible to get travel documents. Her opportunity came when, in 1943, she was approached to be part of the resistance and began training to parachute behind enemy lines. Educated as a soldier, parachutist and intelligence operative, she was eager to begin her mission.

In March of 1944 it was too dangerous to land in German-occupied Hungary, so the team let their silk chutes open over Yugoslavia, plummeted to earth and hid with local freedom fighters until they could slip into Hungary. But Senesh grew impatient; under the cloak of darkness she crept over the border, and was captured in a matter of days.

Despite repeated beatings by her interrogators, Senesh never revealed the details of her mission. She soon found out that, incredibly, her mother was being held at the same camp. Fearing for her mother's safety, Senesh never mentioned her mission.

While other prisoners were being sent off to death camps, Senesh was charged with treason. In court she renounced her Hungarian citizenship and accused Hungary of treason for crimes against its own people. Sentenced to death, she was asked if she sought clemency. She claimed she would never seek leniency from murderers. Unbowed, she died in front of a firing squad at the age of twenty-three.

Emm Gryner and Julia Fordham bond in Toronto.

Was it the fact that Lilith was a chick tour that made it so different? Who can say? Perhaps women ruling the roster made it easier to innovate. Maybe with old standards being cast aside so happily, the status quo was forced to release its stranglehold. With the old rules no longer in place, creativity, and innovation flourished.

This innovation was also expressed when Lilith turned to the women outside of the stage's warm enclave and shared some of the same warmth. After the press conferences, when the cheques were handed over to local women's groups, there often wasn't a dry eye in the house – sometimes even members of the press were caught sniffling.

"When I handed a cheque over to a shelter in Seattle for twenty thousand, the woman who accepted it said it would would keep the shelter open for another year," Sarah states proudly. "That's a pretty wicked feeling. But while I actually handed the cheques over to the charities, each performer had a part in it because their music helped raise that money. And everyone was able to share in those beautiful moments."

This is the spirit that binds Lilith together, that propels the tour from city to city and from dream to reality.

We live in a time and place with so few rites of passage that it's sometimes difficult to enter adulthood with confidence and pride. In fact, some critics have described the state of Western culture as being a sibling society — one in which nobody assumes any responsibility for or offers guidance to our youth. Other writers have suggested that we need to reclaim past traditions in order to help our youth make the sometimes difficult transition into adulthood. One important element of these traditions is that of the mentor or role model, the figure who both serves as a guide and an inspiration.

With so many outspoken women on the Lilith Fair tour, it's not surprising that the term "role model" surfaced during the first full-length run. Sometimes the press raised the subject but, perhaps surprisingly, the performers themselves also broached the topic. They spoke of the need for such guides and wondered if their own lives and careers could be inspirational to others. And sometimes they lamented the lack of role models in their early years.

Aside from mothers and grade school teachers, many of us grew up without a heroine in sight. Yet there's a myriad of women — both living and historical — whose lives are worthy of emulation. For Fiona Apple, inspiration came from the books of

African-American author Maya Angelou. "She was so visibly proud of herself even when she wrote of being humiliated, vulnerable or defeated," says Fiona. This prompted Fiona to dig deep and unearth her own strength. "I read Maya and thought, this woman is so incredible and yet she's been as weak as I feel. That made me think I can be like that. Just because I started out as a weak little victim in a shrink's office doesn't mean I have to finish up that way."

Even with a rich history of remarkable women, many of the performers on Lilith Fair felt rudderless in their youth. Without female role models, they couldn't find the guidance and inspiration they craved. Meredith Brooks, for example, had to teach herself how to play the guitar when still a teenager, simply because she couldn't find a woman instructor. This early experience has led her to consider her own influence. "I feel that I am a necessary inspiration right now. I want to help little girls to grow up knowing they have a right to own their creativity."

Fortunately, female role models are easier to find today than they were twenty years ago. From working mom CEOs to TV's brassy babes, there's a real diversity of female images in the 90s. Of course, while diversity is an important part of role modelling, some of the performers fear it can mean that women have the freedom to be just as screwed up as the boys. "A couple years ago I was at a concert, and I won't say which one or who was playing, but the woman on stage was messed up really bad," comments Kim Fox. "And all these young girls were walking around with her T-shirts on, just as messed up. I sat down and started to cry because I thought this is what our youth is looking up to. Yet, at Lilith Fair, I noticed there was a young crowd that looked really wide-eyed and excited."

The kids Kim saw in the audience seemed dramatically different from those who had prompted her tears a few years before. "They looked happy and really together," she enthuses. "Seeing that felt great and wiped out all those feelings from years ago. I felt proud."

While the Lilith women are aware of their potential as role models, they're also wary of what too much adoration can do to young fans. "Looking to us for guidance is fine," says Jewel, "so long as it isn't idol worship, or *idle* worship, for when you idolize someone you're very stagnant."

What troubles Jewel the most is that some people place her on a pedestal – the object of blind adulation – instead of seeing her as a source of inspiration. This makes her particularly uncomfortable because, role models aside, she feels that the most

Jewel answers questions at The Gorge press conference.

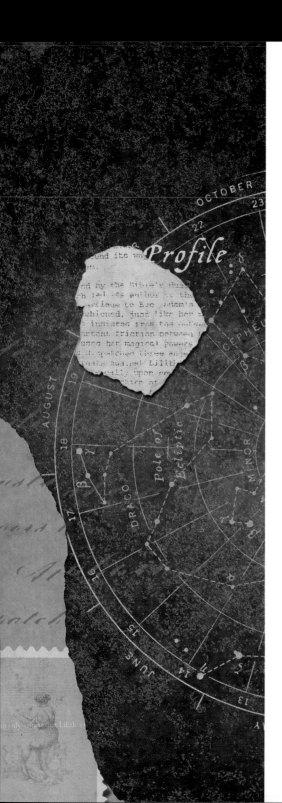

Profile

Hildegarde of Bingen

1089~1179

At a time when the world of a woman often meant little more than hearth and home, some found ways to transcend the limited space in which they spent their days. One such woman was Hildegarde of Bingen. The founder of a convent, this remarkable woman accomplished much within the confines of the convent walls.

Hildegarde was born into a noble family. Because she was the tenth child, she was promised to the church, a common custom in those days. At the age of eight her family sent her off to study with Jutta of Spanheim, an anchoress. When Jutta died, the charismatic Hildegarde was chosen to be the leader of the convent, but the community she created was much different than what you might expect. The position of women in medieval society was often a mute and subservient one but the nuns, free from the scrutiny of men, could explore thoughts and practices usually denied to their sex.

With divine visions that inspired writings, paintings, music and scientific explorations, Hildegarde became one of most important thinkers of her era. Even so, she was often plagued by self-doubt. She once wrote that the reason she refused to write for a long period of time was because of self-doubt and the low opinion she had of herself combined with the disparaging sayings of men. She overcame these fears to write a number of moral plays, theological explorations, scientific dissertations, treatises on natural history, and musical works, the latter of which are seeing a revival today.

Acutely aware of the relationship between spirituality and the natural world, Hildegarde often wrote of what she called *Viriditas* – or greening power – the power which enlivens and encourages creativity and fruitfulness. A mystic, scientist, scholar, musician, composer, philosopher and environmentalist, Hildegarde was way ahead of her time – a renaissance woman long before the Renaissance began.

important thing is to believe in yourself. "You have to know your own truth. Nobody knew mine before me." That doesn't, of course, mean that she hasn't been motivated by the work of others. "It's good to be inspired by people. I've been immensely inspired by women like Tracy Chapman and Anaïs Nin. It's great if their work makes you want to do better. "But," she concludes in a warning tone, "I think it's damaging if it starts making you think these people are doing something you never could."

With a sea of young faces staring up from the world beyond the stage, all the performers are acutely aware of the power they have. And it's this desire to share their experiences with the next generation of women that prompted many of the artists, including Paula Cole, to sign on to the tour. "I believe in what Lilith Fair is doing. I think it's a symbol of hope," says Paula, summing up the feelings of many in a few heartfelt words. "The most interesting achievements of the tour will take place in the lives of the young girls who are coming. I hope that our bonding together as women in music and business will inspire them to do something with their own lives and to stand a little taller."

But it's not just the audience that's standing taller at the end of Lilith Fair. The travelling community that sprang up

Paula Cole

cont.

around the Lilith stage is a powerful teacher and guide for the artists and crew themselves. With a performance roster that spans generations, the opportunity to learn from peers presents itself on a daily basis – whether it's the musical lessons coming from the stage, the personal advice shared in the dressing rooms, or the media savvy discussed before press conferences.

   "What the audience gets out of Lilith is the same thing that I am getting," says up-and coming musician Leah Andreone. "I'm learning from these women. And I think that Lilith teaches about perseverance and that you can overcome what some people say you'll never overcome. When you're a woman you're always told that achieving your goals will be more difficult than if you were a man, and that's true. But obviously," she adds with a triumphant grin, "we've done it!"

Cassandra Wilson at The Gorge press conference.

ertainly it could be said that much of Lilith Fair's appeal lies in its simplicity. Some of the tour's best moments were composed of only three things: a woman, an acoustic guitar and a spectacular voice.

With the Fair boasting so many performers whose work sidesteps pop's flavour-of-the-month fads and whose success relies primarily on their natural gifts and not technological wizardry, you might be tempted to think the tour is free of all the latest bells and whistles. But wait a second. Listen. Is that wheezing and whining coming from a deathly ill singer on a shockingly bad day? Or is it just the telltale sound of two computers connecting?

Another of Lilith's distinguishing characteristics was its pioneering use of multimedia and the Internet. The tour's Web site at www.lilithfair.com received up to 300,000 hits a day and was as much a part of the tour as the performers or crew.

The intent of the site was two-fold: first, it was a clearing house for information about who was touring when and, second, it was a symbol of the community Lilith was trying to create.

"We hoped that this would be a ground-breaking event and we thought it was essential to document every facet of the tour on a daily basis," says Nettmedia Project Manager Cathy Barrett. While the presence of a full film crew to capture the show is probably on the horizon, Lilith '97 was translated to the Web by a dedicated

Chapter Four:

The
Multimedia
is the
Message

multimedia team. Armed with sunscreen, cameras and microphones, information gatherers Cathy Barrett and erstwhile V J Jana Lynn White worked every day of the seven-week tour, while several other enthusiastic colleagues worked on a rotating schedule. "The energy was something I'd never experienced before," says Barrett, who has toured with Sarah in the past. "We tried to capture it through interviews with the performers, crew and members of the audience."

The team came with its own magic bus, decked out with all the shiny toys of the trade: laptops, scanners, digital video cameras and the most important thing – Internet access.

The Internet, being an international phenomenon, hosted a document that could be seen worldwide and also allowed the Nettmedia team to assemble the site from the road. The pages were updated daily, with millions of bytes being pumped over telephone lines back to the server in Vancouver, where the site was hosted. The programming and video editing was done in New York.

"No one had done anything quite like this," says Lane Dunlop, president of Nettmedia and part of the touring multimedia team. "So, we couldn't exactly fall back on what people had done in the past. But Lilith is such an amazing concept, and we didn't want the incredible spirit that was at each show to disappear when the tour moved on. Our goal wasn't to recreate Lilith Fair – that would

Sarah McLachlan being interviewed by Jana Lynn White and Cathy Barrett.

be impossible," he explains. "Instead we wanted to give people a sense of what happened each day."

The immediacy of the Internet allowed people who hadn't seen the tour to still participate. For the fan who wasn't able to come, the Web site was a taste of what they were missing. "We had so much of the tour: video clips from the performances, interviews, and backstage at Juliana Hatfield's 30th birthday party," says Barrett. The Web team urged fans to post online reviews and even encouraged performers to submit tour diaries of their thoughts and drawings.

The site aimed to be a cornucopia of all things Lilith. "There were people who followed the tour via the Web site, and you could actually do that," Barrett adds. "If you were following this day by day, you would actually get to know who was on the road, not just the artists but also even the crew. We hoped the Web site would make people feel like they were part of Lilith Fair."

The site was a place where the tour could be viewed with a minimal amount of intervention, an approach many found refreshing, especially since, in this age of media pervasiveness, we often rely on reporters and other intermediaries to interpret events for us. As Indigo Girl Amy Saliers believes, sometimes the media's hunger for an angle can mean that images of an event are skewed to fit a particular agenda. And, as Lisa Loeb suggested one harried day, the media can even get in the way of the event itself.

Emily Saliers and Amy Ray.

63

While much has been made of the media's treatment of Lilith Fair, no one could say the Fair was left to languish in the shadows. Given the relentless wave of articles and profiles surfacing in papers, magazines and on the airwaves, the tour's profile was so high that you couldn't imagine a journalist asking "Lilith who?"

From the moment that Sarah first announced that she was assembling the tour, the media began to nibble. After the commercial and critical success of Lilith's trials runs in 1996, the snacking ceased – and the feeding frenzy began.

With cover stories in magazines that ran the gamut of press – from *Entertainment Weekly* to MTV to alternative weeklies – the tour took centre stage and tried not to blink in the unrelenting glare of the spotlight.

Considering the size of that spotlight, Lilith's steadfast response was no small feat. The hype surrounding the festival soon reached a maddening din.

Much of the press was positive. *Time*'s cover story on the Fair, featuring Jewel on the front cover of the US edition and Sarah on the front cover of the Canadian one, spoke of its mix of feminism and the feminine. Unlike alternative rock, wrote Christopher John Farley, Lilith "is less about stoking cynicism

Sarah McLachlan reads the news.

and provoking anger than it is about overcoming both…Right now pop is flaccid…and the Lilith tour can help halt pop's garbage chute slide."

Time was only one of the many media voices that lavished praise on the Fair. *Entertainment Weekly* dubbed Lilith "summer's hottest ticket." *Pulse* magazine exclaimed "some of the world's best ideas are not just actions, but reactions. Such is the case with Lilith Fair." And *Performing Songwriter* suggested that the tour "verges on the revolutionary."

Some critics, however, were less sanguine about Sarah's baby. Ann Powers, in an *US* magazine article, began with the line "Sarah McLachlan: Goddess," and wrote about the tour in the same complimentary fashion. But her *Village Voice* review took a decidedly vitriolic turn as she dismissed any feminist integrity the tour may have claimed. "Lilith has no other purpose than the 'celebration' of female artists." wrote Powers, "yet its focus on identity makes it seem like a noble cause. McLachlan," Powers continued, "organized an event in which promoting herself is perceived as a political act. The more famous she is, the better we all feel."

In a blistering *Rolling Stone* article called "Backstage at Lilith," journalist Lorraine Ali painted a picture of Lilith Fair as

petty and utterly lacking in any community, and described
the press conferences as having "an underlying sense of competi-
tiveness, which resembles the uncomfortable alliance of a
NATO meeting."

"That was very unfortunate," says Sarah when reminded
of Ali's piece. "And it's simply not true. For God's sake," she
exclaims, "it was the first week of the tour. Exactly how much
community could she have expected after only a few days? We
were still smoothing out wrinkles! And as far as us communicating
goes, I was having three-hour rant sessions with Paula Cole, but
Ali just didn't see them." She adds wryly, "and we know that if
the media doesn't see it, it didn't happen."

Yet even Ali's piece paled next to the acerbic missive from
the keyboard of Sarah Vowell, music columnist for the Web
magazine *Salon*.

In an article titled "Throwing Ovaries: The Second-
Grade Sensibility of the Pseudo-Feminist Lilith Fair," Vowell
accused Sarah and company of "nailing a pretty pink sign to their
cute clubhouse marked 'NO BOYS ALLOWED.'"

While most of what Vowell wrote seemed more about sexy
copy than fair assessment, she did raise some interesting points.
Her article included a passage from the *Entertainment Weekly*
cover story that quoted Sarah as saying that after years of

Kelly "We love boys here!" Willis.

67

Profile

Hypatia

(370 ‹ 415)

Hollywood has committed many classic tales to celluloid, but there's one story from ancient Alexandria that still eludes the film camera's eye: the story of Hypatia. While many details of her life remain obscured by time, she's become a totem of female power.

Hypatia was the daughter of Theon, one of the most educated men of his day. Theon wanted to raise the perfect human – a well educated and well rounded individual. With this in mind he set about creating Hypatia in the image of that ideal.

As a child, astronomy, astrology, philosophy and mathematics were Hypatia's playthings. As an adult she quickly became a well-known thinker and educator. In her 30s, she took the helm of the most significant intellectual institution of her time, wrote a number of books and academic commentaries, and invented a number of astronomical tools.

Hypatia was no austere academic prude. A dynamic woman in a somewhat sexually liberated time, she had her share of suitors. Once, when the advances of a student were unwelcome, the ever-patient Hypatia urged him to more lofty pursuits. When his passion reached a fevered pitch, Hypatia wasted no time addressing his folly. She hurled a stream of vitriol in his direction – as well as a sanitary napkin – and quickly doused his flame. Clearly, Hypatia was a woman who didn't suffer fools gladly, In fact, it appears that she didn't suffer fools at all.

During Hypatia's life Christianity was on the rise, and both her extensive education and her Pagan faith spawned fear in the locals. Under suspicion of witchcraft, Hypatia was attacked and murdered by an angry mob. Hypatia's death marked the end of truly free thought in the ancient world and ushered in a dark period in women's history, but her memory is a paean to the the spirit of intellectualism and feminism.

women's voices being suppressed, now was a time when they could be heard, loved and respected for what they said. Vowell's response? "I thought we'd come into a time when women can be heard so the world can decide whether or not that individual is worth listening to. Love and respect are always optional."

When the quote was shown to Sarah during the first Lilith tour, she was unfazed. "Absolutely," she agreed. "Love and respect are always optional." For, despite media characterizations, Sarah resisted seeing Lilith as an airy-fairy, let's all get together and love everyone event – although she doesn't think love and respect are bad goals. "But remember that I started a music festival here," she laughed, "not a political campaign."

But Sarah didn't see all of Vowell's column in which the music critic lambasted the Fair for everything from its musical choices, described as "pretty, polite, folksy moderates with sensible hair and more melody than message," to the "nauseating language" of its fund raising categories. The article even dismissed all the performers involved as "cute, nice and not extravagantly smart."

Hearing the quote almost a year later, it's clear that Sarah has grown weary of responding to media attacks. "Ouch," she winced. "Ah, I was so naive about the role of the media darling. I had never been in that position before. I didn't understand that you get pushed up there and then pushed down in the muck. That's the muck."

And what of *Ms.* magazine scolding Sarah for her reluctance to use the word "feminist?" *Ms.*, a bastion of 70s feminism, felt that her references to "extremist feminists" and her assertions that Lilith wasn't about "chopping anyone's dick off" were "narrow, negative assumptions about what feminism means."

Sarah McLachlan smiles through another press conference.

Again, Sarah says her words have been misconstrued, and that her comments about dick-chopping were responses to a daily barrage of questions like "why aren't you including men – do you hate them?" "I'm sure *Ms.* was upset about what I said," she concedes, "but if I took every opportunity to spout feminism then, sadly, men would be terrified of the tour. And in order for Lilith to achieve our goals, we couldn't have it be marginalized."

She's quick to point out that she's never denied being a feminist. "Absolutely, I'm a feminist," she says. "And I don't hate men. I know that it's ridiculous that I have to say those things in the same breath, and I don't want to have to. Yet," she explains, "many people still equate feminism with man-hating. I tried to diffuse that thinking because I don't think that's what feminism is. But," she concedes, "I can't escape what many people still believe it to be."

Profile

Lise Meitner

1878 ≤ 1968

As a young Jewish girl growing up in turn of the century Vienna, Austria, Lise Meitner's head was filled with images of women like Madame Curie and Florence Nightingale. Perhaps it was the strength of these role models that made her dream of university.

After gaining acceptance into the University of Vienna, Meitner threw herself into her scientific studies. Despite often being the lone female in a room full of hostile men, the young scholar's standing was often far above her peers. Although she was a gifted student, she was initially reluctant to push for her doctorate as, after all, only fourteen such degrees had been granted to women in the previous 541 years. But in 1906, a triumphant Meitner pushed that number up by one.

After graduation she went to Berlin to attend a series of lectures and ended up staying in Germany for some thirty years. While Meitner's head was buried in the stuff of electrons and nuclei, the Nazi party took power and Meitner was forced to flee her adopted country.

Her departure from Germany took her to the University of Stockholm and further work in nuclear physics. Informed by the discoveries of scientists like Einstein, Bohr and her old co-worker Hahn, Meitner began researching the concept of nuclear division. Aided by her nephew Otto Frisch, she proved that such a thing was possible. Their landmark paper on the subject was published in 1939.

Meitner's discovery of fission soon led to the production of a nuclear bomb, a project that she played no role in. After the war she resumed her work on subatomic particles, and while she went on to receive a multitude of awards, she was passed over for the most desirable accolade of all, the Nobel Prize, which was given to Hahn.

Sarah McLachlan and Lisa Loeb.

Another topic that Sarah no longer has much patience for is Lilith's musical diversity. Seldom, she points out, do critics address the fact that she invited everyone from Queen Latifah to L7, both of whom declined her 1997 offer. She adds that when critics rebuke the line-up for its "narrow range," they sound exactly like the promoters and DJs who prompted her to start Lilith Fair in the first place.

"It's frustrating to me because I really don't think that Paula Cole and I sound the same. I honestly don't. It's like years ago when Sinéad O'Connor and Tori Amos and myself were all dumped into the same group because we were women, regardless of if we actually made similar music."

However, with Lilith Fair built in an estrogen ghetto, isn't the tour itself guilty of the same charges? "I guess you could say I'm digging myself a bit of a hole," she admits. "Yet, I honestly don't think it's the same thing. I'm taking the ghettoization of women and subverting it – turning it into something positive. And," she adds, "the coverage was largely complimentary."

But the criticism hasn't gone unnoticed, and Sarah has come to realize that she simply can't please everyone all the time. "Therefore," she concludes "you have to remain ruthlessly true to yourself, to your plan and your goals. My goal, and that of my partners, is to put on a good festival with good music."

With the chorus of voices both lauding and lambasting Lilith Fair, it's hard to decide if the festival achieved its goals. Viewed solely from the perspective of the media, Lilith Fair is caught between any number of groups: it's considered too radical by the mainstream, too mainstream by the radicals, too straight by the queers, too queer by the straights, too vacuous by the quasi-intellectuals and too heavy by those who just want to drink beer and listen to some good tunes.

But, if all these people really had problems with the tour, then who bought all the tickets? In the end, it seems that even with verbal battles being fought in the media's coliseum, fans were flocking to Lilith Fair, quite willing to make up their own minds.

Lauren Hoffman, Leah Andreone , Sarah McLachlan, Kim Bingham and Suzanne Vega.

T he travelling caravan of Lilith Fair set up camp in over
thirty cities from its launching pad in George,
Washington to its teary and triumphant conclusion in
Vancouver, British Columbia. Audience members not only
witnessed stirring and sensational performances by a spectrum
of women, but also took part in a musical event that became a
cultural lightning rod – sparking discussions about women that
reached far beyond the parameters of the musical world.

One significant facet of the Fair was that what
transpired offstage was often as important as what happened in
the spotlights. While concert-goers applauded the concept of a
festival with an all-female bill, the Fair's pervasive sense of
pleasure, vindication and validation wasn't exclusive to the
appreciative audience.

Accordingly, some aspects of the Fair are best understood
through the prism of the performers. However, it's not just their
interpretations of the Fair that are important – it's also their
histories. Every performer who appeared at Lilith Fair has a
story to tell, with varying paths of struggle, discrimination,
encouragement, and achievement. Each woman's story is a unique
account of how her musical efforts became the songs that were
heard by thousands of people in the summer of 1997.

Chapter Six:
Retrospective

This is a profile of a small fraction of the participating artists. It illustrates the colourful array of the talent, the characters, the determination and the music that characterized the first Lilith Fair as a rich, precedent-setting musical experience.

Cassandra Wilson

The silken caresses of Cassandra Wilson's voice first cast their magic while she was growing up in Jackson, Mississippi. With music in her blood – her dad was musician Herman Fowlkes – Wilson began playing piano at the age of nine and started writing her own songs shortly after that. While still in her teens, she forged a solid reputation as a folk and jazz singer and performed throughout Mississippi and Arkansas.

Yet when she enrolled in Jackson University, the word "music" was conspicuously absent from her transcript. Wilson tried several different majors including English, Theatre, and Philosophy, before finally earning a degree in Mass Communications. Why no music? Simply because she had been warned that the industry was too difficult. Wilson recalls, "When I was in school I avoided music because my mother told me that I wouldn't be able to make a living at it. I did it to please her. I stayed away from it as long as I could, and I studied really hard,

Sarah McLachlan and Cassandra Wilson at a press conference.

became an A student and I graduated *cum laude* – all the things she wanted me to do. I joined a sorority, got married and after that I went back to music and did what I wanted to do."

It's a good thing Wilson eventually did pursue her love of music; to date she has released ten solo albums and has appeared as a featured vocalist on a slew of others. Wilson's performance style is widely praised as being magnetic, and she has a Grammy to prove it. Citing Billie Holiday and Joni Mitchell as influences, it's no surprise that this eclectic performer effortlessly scales boundaries between musical genres and infuses all she touches with an elegant mix of reverence and insouciance.

Emmylou Harris

With over a quarter century in the business and a six-pack of Grammys on her mantel, Emmylou Harris is quite possibly Lilith Fair's mentor. But praise like that doesn't actually render an image of the woman who has commanded such respect. Perhaps it's better to speak of how with every small motion, from hoisting a guitar strap over her shoulder to shielding her eyes from the sun, Harris has an air about her that defies labels and inspires confidence. She has the ease of a wise woman while exuding an air of vitality.

Emmylou Harris and Bonaparte.

79

Profile

Mary Wollstonecraft
1759-1797

As the mother of Mary Shelley, whose tormented dreams created the gothic tale of Frankenstein, Mary Wollstonecraft's name would be an interesting one to drop even if she weren't the mother of modern feminism.

Wollstonecraft grew up watching her father abuse her mother. It was a sight that guided her life, and determined that she'd never submit to violent servitude. At a time when marriage was the ultimate goal for a woman, Wollstonecraft was openly opposed to the concept, refusing to believe that women should be the chattels of men. She fled her family home and, soon after, in a daring act of defiance, rescued her younger sister from a miserable marriage.

With two friends, Wollstonecraft opened a girls' school, allowing her to act as conduit between her students and the intellectually stimulating clime of the era. It also let her continue her own intellectual development and in 1786 she wrote and published a pamphlet called "Thoughts on the Education of Daughters." She immersed herself in the world of ideas and letters, becoming a magazine critic, and committing herself to social and political activism.

As the French Revolution raged across the English Channel, Wollstonecraft hoped that it would somehow lead to the emancipation of women. But not only did it deny women their freedom, it led to the execution of feminists. Wollstonecraft poured her rage into a book, *Vindication of the Rights of Women*, which became one of the cornerstone texts of the suffrage movement. She wrote that a continued gender inequality would halt the progress of humanity and argued that women deserved the same education as men. "I have thrown down the gauntlet. It is time to restore women to their lost dignity."

Sadly, Wollstonecraft's life of dissent, action and argument was cut short when she died of complications resulting from the birth of her daughter, Mary.

Harris is completely comfortable at centre stage, feeling the glow of the lights like a warm embrace. "I've never had stage fright; I've always felt natural and at home. But," she adds, "as soon as there is a camera, and I'm supposed to be acting or going through a motion I tend to get self-conscious. I think you have to be totally unself-conscious to sing. You have to be totally connected to yourself and totally disconnected at once."

While this seemingly contradictory alignment of self may seem virtually impossible, Harris makes it appear effortless. It's because of this that she has become a symbol of what can be accomplished in the industry. The Nashville-based performer has won a wondrous array of awards, released twenty-five albums, toured all over the world and managed to be politically active and raise children while doing it — and she's nowhere near done.

Fiona Apple

Fiona Apple is barely twenty years old, yet she has stirred up more controversy in her teens than most people do in a lifetime. With tirades against everything from eating Thanksgiving turkey to the vapidness of the music industry, Apple has done more than bite the hand that feeds her — she's damn near lopped it off.

But Apple isn't apologetic, and despite a whirling dervish-like presence when performing, she's decidedly less frenetic offstage. For her, performing is simply a public catharsis: "I spent a lot of my life having all of my catharsis in shrink's offices with someone who didn't really care about me. And maybe these people [the audience] don't care about me, but I think a lot of them do and I certainly care about them. It's just cool to be up there and at least be creative."

Apple feels that while she's the only one who can fight her personal demons, the pain of the battle is worth it if she can use her experience to help others. The least she can do, she figures, is to exercise her creativity in the hopes that someone else can benefit from the struggle.

Tidal, Apple's debut release, fell into the angry young woman bin until critics actually listened to the CD and found themselves spellbound by the force of her work. And now, with millions of albums sold and a media glare that is both illuminating and blinding, Apple has proven herself talented enough to stay afloat, and strong enough to do much more than simply tread water.

Fiona Apple backstage.

Amy Ray and Emily Saliers

Indigo Girls

If you sift through the CD collection of many college-aged North American women, the Indigo Girls are more than likely to be somewhere in the pile. Amy Ray and Emily Saliers, the core of this Atlanta, Georgia-based duo, have managed to achieve success while at the same time being active supporters of social justice in an industry that seems more concerned with profits.

The pair began their careers in Atlanta, a town they still call home. They formed their first band together while still in high school and, within a few years, the Indigo Girls brought home their first of several Grammys.

The all-female vibe of Lilith Fair is nothing new to these women. As long-time supporters of women's music festivals, they have often shared bills with other female performers, and it's the sense of community at such events that moves them.

"Every person that we've come across has had something musically that I can pick up," says Ray. "My favourite day," she adds, "was the day we were in the dressing room and Jewel came in and taught us how to yodel, Sheryl Crow came in and learned how to play a song with us and played accordion, and Shawn Colvin started teaching us 'Acadian Driftwood.' Everyone came to the dressing room in one day and it was the moment when everything culminated." For Ray, it was then that she knew what the tour was all about.

That sense of purpose and community was also clear to Saliers. As she recalls, "That fact that Lilith donated a dollar from each ticket sale to women's groups, and seeing the reactions of the women heading up the centres was a powerful experience, as powerful as anything else. The women would often weep openly because they didn't expect that the cheques were going to be that big. And we would sniffle and think, this is why we're here."

Jewel

Most people's image of Alaska is a barren one – a landscape of snow, ice and little else. In truth it's the land of the midnight sun, a world of breathtaking summer foliage and the much-loved home of Jewel Kilcher.

Jewel began singing at the tender age of five. Through her formative years she did little shows for tourists and this eventually led to a scholarship at Interlochen Fine Arts Academy in Michigan. After she graduated, she packed up her dreams and moved to San Diego with her mother.

It was there that she paid her dues, playing three-hour sets in coffeehouses and working long hours. But when the compromises of work became too great, she moved into her VW van so she could write songs without worrying about what she'd have to do to pay the bills.

The time spent cloistered in the confines of her van spawned *Pieces of You*, her multi-platinum debut which snagged her a bevy of Grammy nominations and firmly established her as a promising young artist.

With a torrent of media attention storming around her, the young Jewel remains remarkably centred. The one thing she dislikes about her new life is the lack of silence. "We can't underestimate the value of silence," says the affable Jewel. "We need to create ourselves, need to spend time alone. If you don't," she adds, "you risk not knowing yourself and not realizing your dreams."

Jewel has already realized many of her dreams, and with a leading role in Ang Lee's new film as well as a collection of poetry in the works, she's seeing many more dreams come true. And while she enjoys the positive aspects of her success, she remains keenly aware of what's not right in the world around her.

"I see how we rob each other's dignity all the time, like not giving money to someone 'cause you think they'll drink. It's not your job to judge. Like being rude to people in a grocery store if they take too long to give you your change. Tolerance, and patience," she asserts, "is how the world changes."

And with this attitude, the multifaceted Jewel manages to maintain a realistic view of the way things work without being bound by the sadness that grim reality often delivers. "After all," she suggests, "you can't fight the enemy with despair."

Joan Osborne

Having shared stages with the likes of Stevie Wonder, Luciano Pavarotti and the late Nusrat Fateh Ali Khan in the last three years alone, it almost sounds like Joan Osborne rode into fame effortlessly. But it's only after years of belting out her soulful notes in bars throughout New York that she achieved commercial success with the album *Relish* and the single, "One of Us."

In fact, Osborne has just released a testament to those difficult years, a collection called *Joan Osborne: Early Recordings*. These songs were originally released on her own boldly named record label, Womanly Hips, a name which indicates that there's more to Osborne than just another pretty voice. Christening her label this way suggests that she is comfortable enough with her own body and sexuality to challenge stereo-typical images of women.

Profile

Murasaki Shukibu
10th – 11 c

❧ **In a world filled with millions** of novels it's difficult to imagine a time when the writing of one was considered a novel act. The first novel blossomed in the mind of a Japanese woman whose real name is not known, but who is called Murasaki Shukibu.

Born to a governor and scholar, Shukibu's keen thinking revealed itself at a young age. However, she soon learned that the quality of a woman's thought was of little importance to most. Fortunately, her father encouraged her intellectual development and allowed Shukibu to join her brother in his studies. Then, in her twenties, the imperial family of Japan brought Shukibu into the high court as a lady in waiting to the Empress Akiko.

Women were forbidden to write in Chinese script, which Shukibu had mastered, as it was considered the domain of men. The Empress, however, was impressed with Shukibu's abilities and asked Shukibu to teach her how to read and write in Chinese. The lessons had to be conducted in secret for fear of being caught.

During this time Shukibu wrote the first novel. Called *The Tale of Genji*, it depicts the lives of those who lived in the high court. Like all Japanese women at the time, Shukibu was completely cut off from the power structure of the aristocracy and sheltered from the realities of public life. The book is the offspring of her diary writings about court life – a world she often found frivolous and tiresome.

Spanning fifty-four chapters and covering seventy-five years of the fictional Prince Genji's life, it is considered to be the world's first psychological thriller.

Shukibu's book became wildly popular. A brilliant illustration of Japan's Heian period, many critics believe that *The Tale of Genji* is one of the finest books in the Japanese literary canon.

Joan Osborne and Katell Keineg.

Osborne concurs. "One thing that I would like to be able to do is to expand the parameters of what is considered to be attractive or beautiful or media-worthy. I don't really look like most women who are on TV and I fall outside of that narrow confine of what's considered beautiful by our culture. So it's gratifying when I can stand on a stage and feel very powerful and beautiful because I am doing my music, and people can realize that not everyone has to look a certain way to be beautiful."

But Osborne didn't always possess this lack of anxiety about the way she looks. She recalls, "I used to be very shy and under the spell of that cultural conditioning that says you have to look a certain way. What music did was allow me to lose that self-consciousness and find real strength, power and connectedness with something that was larger than myself. And if I can spread that around – to let people be aware that a connection to something is what makes you beautiful – that's definitely worth doing."

Lisa Loeb

With an impish air and a pair of kitsch horn-rims balanced on her grinning face, Lisa Loeb looks like she might be the girl next door to Beaver Cleaver. But just remember: it's the look that's retro, not the girl.

Loeb is very much a woman of the 90s, but she began her musical career much as any girl in the 50s would have, in front of a row of gleaming black and white keys. And it was there at the piano bench that Loeb created her first compositions. While Loeb laments the painfully autobiographical nature of these early songs, she remains an ardent fan of honesty in music.

"I think music has taught me that being honest is a good thing," says Loeb. "That, through songs, little by little I am learning to be more honest. To be emotional and vulnerable is okay and it actually becomes a strength when you can show that."

She began exploring this vulnerability while still in university by playing music with her roommate. The lure of studies waned and Loeb began to pursue music in earnest, moving to New York City to form her band Nine Stories. Shortly after her arrival in New York she released an acoustic tape which sold like hotcakes at her small shows. But when Loeb's single "Stay" made it on to the soundtrack of the film *Reality Bites*, her career went off like a firecracker.

Loeb then began touring extensively, often accompanied only by her acoustic guitar. After this solitary experience, touring with a large group of women was both welcome and educational.

Lisa Loeb smiles for the Nettmedia camera.

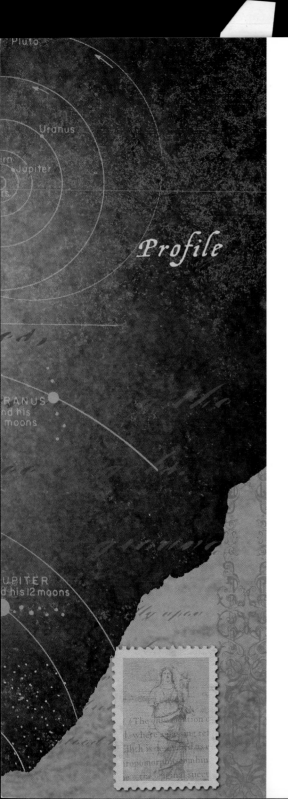

Profile

Nellie McClung
1873≈1951

❧ Canada in the 1800s wasn't exactly the best place for a high-spirited girl like Nellie Mooney McClung. While she longed to play games with the boys at town picnics, the possibility of skirts flying up effectively removed all girls from the games. The role of women, she discovered, was to wait on the sidelines with beverages for the men.

But as any good Canuck knows, Nellie didn't stay on the sidelines for long. While still in her teens she left her home in Ontario, opting for teacher's college in Winnipeg, Manitoba. But it is as a writer and social activist, not a schoolmarm, that McClung is known today.

Women's suffrage was her primary battle, one she attacked with a fury. She wanted to change Canadian legislation that used the word "man" when referring to an individual. Yet, the villain wasn't really the language of the law – it was the men who used syntactical sleight of hand to twist the law to their advantage. They argued that since only men were considered persons under the law, only men were legally eligible to vote. Besides, they told her, nice women don't want the vote.

In 1915, McClung and the Political Equality League responded by staging a mock parliament. They debated men's right to vote, spoke about how nice men didn't want the vote, and lampooned other ridiculous arguments used against the suffragettes.

In 1927, Nellie McClung and four other Canadian women, known as the Valiant Five, demanded that the Supreme Court of Canada declare women persons. Denied at first, the group remained undaunted and appealed to the British Privy Council. The Council described the legislation as "a relic of days more barbarous than ours" and overturned the Canadian decision. On October 18, 1929, McClung, her allies and all Canadian women rejoiced when the court made its ruling: women were indeed persons under Canadian law.

"Music brings people to you," Loeb notes. "It reminds me how important a community is. Something like this Fair reminds me that everyone has their own individual qualities that make us different from each other. Although we should celebrate that we're all women and we're all making music, this brings the differences to light even more. And differences are important."

Mary Chapin Carpenter

Since Mary Chapin Carpenter easily comes across as the kind of performer you can chat with over coffee, it's hardly shocking that *Newsweek* magazine dubbed her "everywoman."

Born in New Jersey and raised all over, Carpenter earned a BA in American Civilization in Washington DC, but resisted putting her college degree to work. Instead, Carpenter opted to test her musical mettle in bars throughout the city and soon landed a recording contract with Columbia Nashville. The rest, as they say, is history. She's picked up a host of awards and accolades in the last ten years, and continues to cut a wide swath through musical genres and boundaries.

In addition to her Grammys and platinum albums, Carpenter has written a children's book, contributed to a collection of essays commemorating American suffrage and is a devout environmentalist and human rights activist. But to congratulate her on her activism is to invite a barrage of disclaimers. Carpenter comments, "I just feel like my cup overflows," and as such, she feels that she can never do enough for these causes.

"The hardest part," laments Carpenter, "is having to say no because you're stretched out. I want to feel like I am not gratuitously involved and I want to be able to really have a concrete impact. When I know I can't, I say no. But I know that I am just one of a gazillion people out there, and I know I don't deserve any special credit. I consider it a privilege that anyone pays attention to what I say."

Modesty aside, part of the reason she's involved with Lilith is because of its sense of community and social responsibility. Carpenter explains, "I feel like I am surrounded by a lot of like-minded individuals who have discovered how easy it is to merge what you love – in this case music – with what's important to you as a concerned citizen of your community and of the world at large."

Mary Chapin Carpenter and Sarah McLachlan in press conference.

Meredith Brooks

Meredith Brooks

Not every woman would be comfortable building her reputation on being a bitch. But Meredith Brooks wasn't trying to win friends with her hit song "Bitch" — she was trying to make a point.

"I'm not there to shame people. I'm there to wake them up a bit," comments Brooks. "If 'Bitch' were the last song anybody ever heard from me I'd be proud. I love the fact that I told the truth finally and that I wasn't afraid to say, 'Okay, I am a bitch sometimes but that's just one tiny element of who I am.'"

Much of her current thinking about identity is informed by the work of her hero Carl Jung, a psychotherapist who wrote of integrating selves. Brooks has devoted herself to recognizing all the different selves that she possesses and to value each on its own merits, a concept that is reflected in her songwriting.

While the discussion of her multiple selves gets plenty of ink, her guitar playing is largely ignored. In fact, Brooks finds herself having to speak out about this oversight far more than she ever thought she would have to. "I see someone like Johnny Lang come out and get four pages in the same guitar magazine that I'm getting four or two paragraphs in, and hardly any of that is about my guitar playing," she muses. "All this when I spend months designing sounds."

Achieving recognition as a guitar player is a never-ending battle for Brooks, who comments, "I've had video directors ask me to set it down in videos or use it as a prop yet I've been playing guitar my entire life and I've worked hard at this. There are a lot of good singer-songwriters out today but there aren't a lot of female guitar players around. It's intimidating when you can't even find a female to learn from. I think we're ready for a woman guitar hero," concludes Brooks, "and I am ready to be that."

Nina Persson

With the release of "Lovefool," The Cardigans escaped the long shadow of famous fellow Swedes, ABBA, and took their place in the spotlight. Showcasing a performance style that is at once cool and kitsch, the group's lead singer Nina Persson is often the focus of media attention, but not always in a way that pleases her.

"Very often in interview situations they talk about our music with the guys and with me they want to know about designers and make-up, things I really hate to talk about," complains Persson. "So I have to interrupt their conversation if I want to say anything about the music. It is an underestimation of how much of a clue I have."

Paula Cole and fans.

A Swedish thumbs-up from Nina and Lasse of The Cardigans.

But as Persson's involvement in songwriting increases, the media may encounter even more resistance from her when using such tactics. Persson wrote about half the lyrics on the album, which didn't come about simply because the singer discovered another mode of expression; rather, she felt it was an artistic necessity.

"I felt that I needed to have more input. I had been singing someone else's lyrics for so long and I just couldn't connect to them. It's fine to a certain extent but as we knew we were going to be touring with this album for a long time, I thought, 'you better know what you are taking about.'"

"I think the music for this album suited my way of thinking," she concludes. "It felt time."

Paula Cole

On the cover of *This Fire*, seven-time Grammy nominee Paula Cole is swinging naked through flames. It's a bold image, one of confidence and perseverance, and is far different from the depiction of the woman who cast her eyes downward on the cover of her debut release, *Harbinger*. Cole made her first album after moving to California and falling into a depression, which is clearly reflected in the lyrics. While *Harbinger* is an evocative and beautiful work, it's populated with characters wracked by self-doubt and a need to escape notice. But escaping notice is certainly something Cole is no longer able to do. With the release of *This Fire*, the Rockport, Massachusetts native has left behind the doubts of her earlier album and come through the fire all the stronger.

So what freed Cole from the uncertainties of the ominously named *Harbinger*? A significant change came from performance itself; after the album's release she toured as a backup vocalist for Peter Gabriel and suddenly went from writing songs in solitude to performing in front of 60,000 people.

It was there that she found her strength. Cole reflects, "I had to become larger than I had learned to be. I think inside, I've always been large, like we are when we're children. When you observe children they don't really have a lot of fear, they're so open to new situations."

One of the reasons Cole chose to tour with Lilith Fair is that she wanted to help the younger generation sidestep the insecurities of her own adolescence. She views Lilith as a symbol of hope, a strong example of community spirit that can translate into the lives of the young faces she sees in the audience. For them, Cole wishes, "I hope that our bonding together as women in music and business will inspire them to do something with their own lives, and to stand a little taller."

Profile

Rani Lakshmibai
(1830≈1857)

꧁ Like the holy river she was named after, the legacy of Manikarnika runs deeply through Indian lore. Better known as Rani Lakshmibai, this 19th-century rebel is remembered for her efforts to wrest the jewel from England's crown.

Manikarnika was born into a high-caste family in British-ruled India. Unlike many women of her era, she was taught to read and write. She also tomboyed with her brothers, learning how to ride horses and handle weapons while at their side.

Soon a marriage proposal appeared from the Maharajah of Jhansi. With her nuptials came a new name: Maharani Lakshmibai – or just Rani. Sadly, the couple's first child, a boy, died when he was three months old. The pair adopted a child, but happiness was short-lived; the Maharajah died shortly after in 1853.

According to Hindu law, their adopted son would be the next Maharajah of Jhansi. The boy was still a minor, so Rani decided to rule Jhansi until he came of age. But the Governor-General of India declared that since the boy was adopted, he wasn't the Maharajah's legal heir, so Jhansi was to be annexed by Britain.

Rani protested immediately. When her appeal to London was denied, she recruited an army some 14,000 strong and prepared for what would be the first armed Indian uprising against British rule. Despite her efforts the British took Jhansi in just two weeks.

Rani Lakshmibai died in battle at the age of twenty-eight. Her body was cremated and buried, and with this she was transported in history, a symbol of the struggle for autonomy for both women and the Indian people.

Shawn Colvin

With the release of *A Few Small Repairs*, Shawn Colvin penetrated the public's consciousness with "Sunny Came Home," and upped her Grammy count to three. With all the sudden attention does Colvin fear that she's simply the media's flavour of the month?

"It doesn't really sink in that way," says the very centred Colvin, "because that's okay with me. I've been doing what I am doing for so long and I am happy with the way it's been. So I don't care if I'm the flavour of the month. It will come and it will go and I will still have this loyal audience that's good to me. I made peace with that a while back, that I didn't need the 'big thing' to happen."

But it did happen. *A Few Small Repairs* is multiple-platinum and Colvin has become a bona fide celebrity after almost twenty years in the business. "When 'Sunny Came Home' first started doing well I went through some existential angst about it," admits Colvin. "I was looking at the numbers and thinking what does this mean? And what it means is you got lucky, that something lined up."

And while her fourth album is the first of her ventures to hit platinum, the seasoned performer has been impressing the folk

circuit for years, building a roster of fans including noted
feminist Gloria Steinem.

Given such overwhelming accolades, some performers
might opt to retreat from their fans. But as a music lover herself,
Colvin is well acquainted with the phenomenon.

"I can identify with fans because I am a fan and was an
avid concert goer," Colvin admits. "I went to shows of people I
adored. It's hard to take in that I am one of those people now. That
I give someone something that's akin to what I got from any
number of people that I loved. It feels good."

Sheryl Crow

With the release of *Tuesday Night Music Club*, Missouri
native Sheryl Crow was catapulted into the international
spotlight and heralded as an overnight success. But dubbing her
an instant sensation is hardly just, especially considering that
Crow moved to LA to pursue a musical career some ten years
before her debut album was released.

After years spent singing backup for stars like Michael
Jackson, Sting and Stevie Wonder as well as having her work
recorded by other artists, including Eric Clapton and Wynonna
Judd, Crow finally decided to focus her talents on her own career;

Sheryl Crow

Rosa Parks

1913 ‑

On the surface it seemed like a harmless thing to do: on December 1, 1955 in Montgomery Alabama, an exhausted Rosa Parks refused to give up her bus seat to a white man. Parks often said of the incident that she had no intention of changing the course of history; rather, after a long day of working as a seamstress, she just wanted to rest.

Parks was sitting in a section of the bus usually used by blacks, but whites were given priority to use those seats when the front rows of the bus were full. That day the front seats filled quickly, so a white man demanded that the middle rows be cleared. Everyone moved to the back of the bus except a silent Parks, who remained seated. Even when the driver threatened to call the police, this usually well-mannered woman didn't move.

Parks was arrested and thrown into jail. She was allowed one phone call, which she made to a lawyer who was with the National Association for the Advancement of Colored People (NAACP).

News of her arrest spread through the town like wildfire. The black community debated what to do in response to her situation; while some advocated a simple boycott, others like Martin Luther King Jr., saw the situation as an opportunity to fight segregation. The black community rallied together and told the city they would boycott the bus system until the law was changed. The boycott lasted over a year, until the US Supreme Court ruled against the city's legislation.

Everyday acts of resistance can be revolutionary, no matter how insignificant they seem at the time. Park's refusal to move, or to pay a fine for disobeying a city ordinance, demonstrates the kind of strength and courage that does more than change bylaws; it changes history.

Amy Ray and Sheryl Crow jam during "Closer To Fine."

consequently, she spent two years writing songs and playing with other musicians in weekly Tuesday evening sessions. The work crafted during this difficult time finally materialized on her debut release, *Tuesday Night Music Club*, which went on to sell millions of copies and garnered Crow widespread media acclaim and a staggering fan base.

Fame did exact its price, however, as the burdens of touring, interviews and video shoots left little time left for pleasure of any kind, let alone bonding with her peers. As Crow explains, "People think that because we're all musicians and that we are all at a certain level we must know each other, and that's not the case."

Fortunately, Lilith allowed for an experience different from other tours. During Crow's stay with Lilith, the veteran performer quickly sensed a different vibe; a vibe she explains on several levels: "Obviously the female camaraderie and the sense of community is a lot different here. Usually on festival tours people just show up before their slot. At Lilith people are getting here early in the morning just to hang out. And as I was leaving last and all the buses were leaving together, people were lined up along the road. Men and women were actually cheering the buses as they went by. You never see that."

Suzanne Vega

Although Suzanne Vega is often perceived as a shy waif, she finds this image consistently at odds with the life she has actually led. The eclectic mix of her cultural education in a community of writers and artists helped build Vega as the consummate image of a coffeehouse performer: introspective, sometimes ethereal, and often precious. However, having grown up on the rough streets of New York's Spanish Harlem in a rather untraditional environment, Vega sees herself quite differently: a chick who grew up on the rough side of town and who works in a music tradition quite different from the disparate and disjointed sounds of the Top 40.

Her songwriting is nearer to poetry than the traditional rhyme schemes of pop, with lyrics that have more kinship with storytelling than distraction. Yet she's explored a variety of music genres from folk to pop, and with her album *99.9F°* she even created a sound that some critics dubbed "industrial folk."

As part of Lilith Fair's trial run in 1996, Vega had a sense of what the tour would blossom into. She recalls, "I suspected it might be this big. I thought it made all the sense in the world." And although Vega was more than a little nervous about returning to the stage after a protracted absence, Lilith Fair felt right for her. As Vega notes, she appreciated Lilith's progressive

Suzanne Vega

Tracy Bonham

philosophical foundation: "I liked the idea of having all women on the same bill and having that be a positive thing rather than the negative thing some promoters would have you believe."

Tracy Bonham

When Tracy Bonham's debut release, *The Importance of Being Upright*, first began edging up radio station playlists, she was a little disappointed with the response. It wasn't that the critics didn't like the classically trained violinist turned singer/songwriter's impressive CD; it was that they pigeonholed her as merely another Alanis Morissette.

Bonham was initially incensed by these references and expressed her frustration with the critics: "I knew it was just a timing thing because she blew up and anyone else who came in after her was inevitably going to be lumped in with her. It was maddening and I dealt with that in almost very interview for a year and a half."

Despite the infuriating comparisons, it soon became clear Bonham wasn't trying to cash in on some angry young woman trend that followed Morissette's success. Bonham had been immersed in the language of music since she was a very young child, when her music-teacher mom suggested she take up the violin. From the moment she first cradled the instrument under her chin, it was clear that music would be her guide.

The promise of the young violinist quickly became visible and a scholarship lifted Bonham from her Eugene, Oregon hometown to the University of Southern California. She later transferred to Boston's Berklee School of Music to study voice as well as violin. But as her studies progressed, the glow of classical music dimmed and Bonham began to speak in a rock vocabulary, soon becoming a fixture on Boston's music scene.

Since then, Bonham has been recognized on her own merits: her candid lyrics, her incisive fiddling and her frenetic performance style. And rightly so – with such an arsenal of tools at her disposal, any rote comparison seems more lazy than savvy.

Victoria Williams

Victoria Williams became something of a household name with the 1993 release of *Sweet Relief*, an album of Williams' compositions recorded by well-known musicians such as Pearl Jam, Michelle Shocked, Soul Asylum, and Matthew Sweet. Ironically, it was her diagnosis with a serious illness that prompted this recognition. When Williams' health was impaired by multiple sclerosis in 1992, she was faced with huge medical

Suzanne Vega in her pint-sized trailer.

bills and, like many American musicians, had no health insurance to cover these expenses. As a result, her friends and fans in the music community rallied together to pay tribute to her songwriting craft and to raise money for her health care.

Before she fell ill, Williams had released two critically acclaimed albums containing her signature quirky vocals and clever, unpretentious songwriting. In her songs, Williams assumes the role of a gifted storyteller, entering the realm of wide-eyed amazement while still acknowledging an awareness of the realities taught to us by some of life's darker lessons. And, although they may sound a bit unusual to unsuspecting ears, her sweet, warbling vocals add another dimension of character to the songs.

Fortunately, Williams is not about to let MS put an end to her music career. Williams is determined to make the most of her talent despite the effects of the illness. For instance, when the acoustic guitar became too difficult for her weakened hands to manage, Williams switched to electric rather than giving up. And her positive attitude continues to infuse her songs with the visionary, transcendent quality that is apparent in *Musings of a Creekdipper*, her second release since she became ill.

Victoria Williams and her band.

Williams' buoyant spirit, friendly songs, and desire to bring joy and understanding into people's lives make her a natural for Lilith Fair. As Williams commented, "It's such a wonderful spirit of togetherness and support. It's a perfect way to enter the 21st century – women's voices getting heard." And considering Williams' struggle to survive in a male-centric industry – she was released from an early development deal with EMI because, as she explains, they already had Kate Bush on the label – having her unique, inspirational voice heard is no small victory.

Of course, these were not the only women that participated in Lilith Fair, but their profiles help represent the brilliant tapestry of this tour. And what a tapestry it was! Beyond the vague recollections of each tour date, there are hundreds of memories and fragments of history for performers and fans alike. From the backstage jamborees to the trail of tour buses leaving the venues, each woman's story is a snapshot of a summer marked by great music, and infused with feelings of pride, camaraderie and hope.

After a final rainy day in Vancouver, Lilith '97 rolled up its backdrop for the last time. A culmination of all the friendships that had sprung up over the summer tour, the teary parting embraces were difficult to end.

Yet as soon as the leaves began to turn, the Lilith Team began to wonder what to approach next. Well, how about a holiday show in West Palm Beach, Florida?

"It was really hard to do a one-off show," said Sarah during the holiday show's press conference, "but we wanted to have a bridge between the tours. Remember," she emphasized, "it's not a preview of the summer show, just a bridge."

The bridge they built was certainly no jerry-rigged affair. The Florida stage held the undeniable talents of Lilith Fair vets like Sheryl Crow and the Indigo Girls as well as newcomers K's Choice, Missy Elliot, Luscious Jackson, and even a comedienne, Saturday Night Live's Ana Gasteyer, there to spoof the show.

While Sarah insisted the Florida show was no preview, it certainly offered a glimpse of what's in the works for Lilith '98. "We got so many of the people we tried to get last year. We have Missy Elliot, Erykah Badu, Queen Latifah, Bonnie Raitt, Natalie Merchant, Sinéad O'Connor, Me'shell Ndegéocello,

Valerie Leulliot of Autour De Lucie.

Neneh Cherry and Luscious Jackson…" she says excitedly. With the dynamic line-up, Sarah was quick to point out that the Orlando show is consistent with the goals Lilith has always had. "I want to make sure people know that this isn't some sudden scramble for diversity," she adds, "it's just that more people said yes this year."

But isn't Sarah concerned that such a wildly diverse group of performers will alter the Fair's already successful vibe? "Absolutely," emphasizes Sarah. "I think it will change in a positive way. We live in such bubbles when we're on the road that it's great to have a mix of people and music on the tour. I think that it will broaden all of our minds."

What about last year's promise to have men in the line-up in the future? "Well," Sarah hesitates, "that was just an idea, a passing fancy I made the mistake of bringing up in a press conference. Then – bam – it was written in stone." Sarah does admit that she seriously considered this possibility, but a number of women on the tour, including Emmylou Harris, said, hey, it works, don't mess with it. "Emmylou pulled me aside and said 'Look, it may not be my place to say this, but why do you want to change anything? It's perfect the way it is.' Besides," Sarah adds, "there are already more men on Lilith than women, and they have all those other festivals," Sarah laughs. "It's not like they won't get to play."

When Lilith began, much of its innovation sprang from swimming in uncharted waters. Now with the authority of a successful tour behind them, will the innovation end? "Absolutely not," says Lilith partner Terry McBride. "That's one of the great things about this show, the opportunity to try out ideas. Chances are that if it's practical, it will get done."

One of the things organizers are doing is renewing their commitment to having local talent play the side stages. "That entails listening to about 3,000 cassettes and CDs, even putting on talent contests in sixteen cities to find local performers," adds McBride. "Do we *need* to do this? Absolutely not. But the principle of it is great. Who knows? Maybe one or two will get discovered and go on to have great careers."

It's clear that while countless ideas are whirring through the heads of everyone at Lilith, the upcoming tour hopes to preserve the magic of last year, and organizers see the future as an opportunity to grow rather than transform.

As festival co-organizer Marty Diamond says, Lilith '98 isn't about reinventing the wheel. "We've been through a maturation process, a growth process. Lilith is a living breathing

Garrison Starr fields questions at press conference.

Profile

Sojourner Truth
1797–1893

✤ Sojourner Truth was born a slave in upstate New York. In 1828, she was granted her freedom by the New York State Anti-Slavery Act. Shedding her slave name of Isabella, she chose her new name carefully: "Sojourner" meaning one who dwells temporarily, and "Truth" for the truth about slavery she intended to share with the world. She took her new found liberty along the eastern seaboard, telling her story as she went, furthering the abolitionist movement, and becoming one of America's most disruptive and dynamic political activists.

Although unable to read or write, Sojourner was an engaging public speaker. During her travels she became aware of the struggle for women's emancipation, a struggle that closely paralleled the abolitionist movement, which had no female leaders. Soon, her speeches about emancipation applied as much to women as they did to blacks. At the 1851 Women's Rights Convention in Akron, Ohio, Sojourner stepped up to the podium and delivered, off the cuff, her famous "Ain't I a Woman?" speech. "Look at me! Look at my arm! I have plowed, I have planted and I have gathered into barns. . . and ain't I a woman?" In response to a remark that women should not have as many rights as men because Christ was a man, she demanded, "Where did your Christ come from? From God and a woman! Man had nothing to do with him!"

Over six feet tall, Sojourner's presence was so commanding that she was often accused of being a man dressed up as a woman. It is said that she once bared her breasts at a meeting to put a stop to such claims.

Aided by a friend, she published her autobiography, *The Narrative of Sojourner Truth*, the proceeds of which allowed her to buy a home and continue her work. She died in her 80s in Battle Creek, Michigan.

thing. People talk about building events or festivals. We didn't build this. It grew and it continues to grow."

So when the final show has come and gone, after all the performers have taken their last bows and the crowd is quietly slipping out of the venue, what remains? Is there anything that continues to resonate after the last notes have died away?

The conception, and subsequent success, of Lilith Fair has been hailed as an important moment in music history. It has also been dismissed as a simply being a savvy business venture. People on each end of this argument may be missing the point: that they're both right.

First, Lilith was a watershed event in contemporary musical history. While it certainly wasn't the first chick festival, it was definitely was the first tour. And while it's true that the Fair didn't cause women to climb the charts, it did recognize that the growing popularity and success of music by women was something to celebrate. By organizing a tour of such magnitude, Sarah McLachlan, her team and everyone involved with the event sent out the message that female musicians aren't going to fade away. Perhaps Lilith's success will prompt people to realize that women's musical successes aren't necessarily about fads. Their victories are testaments to a musical tradition that

Lilith crew members gather for a group picture in Vancouver, BC.

reaches back to include women like Joni Mitchell, Ella Fitzgerald — and even Hildegarde.

Second, Lilith was also undeniably a tremendous commercial success. Over 700,000 people attended the thirty-seven shows in the first Lilith Fair and, between ticket sales, merchandise and associated profits, the tour raked in something to the tune of $750,000 for assorted charities.

In short, it was both a musical first and a savvy business endeavour – there's really no conflict. Part of the reason Lilith Fair is musically significant is precisely because it is a mainstream, successful event. Only from the centre stage of pop music could a message about marginalized women's voices actually be heard. As another female singer/songwriter might say, isn't it ironic?

The spirit of the 1997 Lilith Fair continues to flourish. For truly, there is a spirit here, one that battles with irony and cynicism and hopes to make a better world while doing it. Artists may aim for success, and their career aspirations may have them burning the candle at both ends, but what inspires them to light the match rather than curse the darkness?

Maybe it's the most naive thing of all: the wish for a better tomorrow. Be it music, literature, film, dance or theatre,

Dan Fraser and Sarah McLachlan thank the Lilith crew in Vancouver, BC.

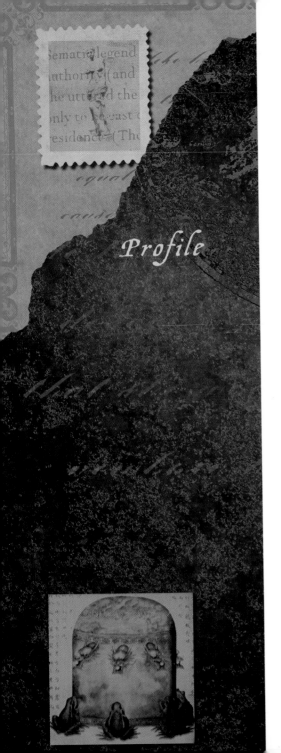

Profile

Trung Trac and Trung Nhi
1st century

◦◦◦ **In everyday conversation,** the word sibling is usually followed by the word rivalry. When we hear of two sisters in battle, we often assume that they're fighting each other. Yet in first century Vietnam, the Trung sisters – Trung Trac and Trung Nhi – fought side by side against Chinese oppressors. The duo were bound by blood and adversity, and the battles they fought have made them Vietnamese folk heroines.

Born into nobility nearly 2,000 years ago, the Trung sisters grew up during a period of Chinese occupation, from which the Vietnamese people suffered greatly. Vietnam had been occupied for nearly two hundred years, so there was little resistance to the foreign presence. But things changed in 39 AD, when a Chinese commander brutally raped Trung Trac and murdered her husband. For Trung Trac, mourning was a luxury in which she did not indulge. Instead, she made a solemn vow: "Foremost, I will avenge my country. Second, I will restore the Hung lineage. Third, I will avenge the death of my husband. Last, I vow that these goals will be accomplished."

With her sister beside her, Trung Trac called upon her people to fight back against the Chinese. They formed an army of 80,000 men and women, among them thirty-six women generals – including the mother of the two sisters. In just a matter of months the army reclaimed sixty-five cities which the sisters ruled as co-sovereigns.

Sadly, the valiant revolt of the Trung sisters was only a short exception to what would become a thousand years of Chinese rule. The Chinese reclaimed the land from the rebels and the sisters chose death over surrender. Both women have become symbols of courage and resistance in Vietnam, and each year the country celebrates the memory of these brave warriors – who just happened to be women.

art is often propelled by vehement hopefulness. Even the most disturbing work, that which draws you into darkness or despair, is inextricably bound to simpler, more lighthearted efforts. They're linked by the shared hope that tomorrow will indeed come and that, perhaps, they may play a role in shaping it.

The aim of Lilith Fair is to balance the scales of power in the music industry and to create a future where an all-woman tour won't be "pioneering" or "ground-breaking" anymore. While Lilith Fair currently wears those words with pride and confidence, its goal is to hasten to an era when the title "musician" is title enough.

From *ilith Fair*

Index

A
Apple, Fiona 3, 53, 54, 82
Askew, Joy 46
B
Bonham, Tracy 35, 44, 108
Brooks, Meredith 14, 54, 96
C
Carpenter, Mary Chapin 94
Carter Harrison, Roberta 45
Chapman, Tracy 4, 58
Charities 27
    ANAD 30
    IRSA 30
    Lifebeat 27
    RAINN 27
    selection of 30
    Strang Cornell Breast Center 27
    WOW 30
Cole, Paula xi, 18, 19, 32, 35, 58, 67, 74, 98
Colvin, Shawn 47, 84, 102
Crow, Sheryl 14, 47, 103, 113
G
Gentileschi, Artemisia 16
Goldman, Emma 41
H
Harris, Emmylou 79, 114
Hypatia 69
I
Indigo Girls 2, 38, 39, 46, 63, 84, 113
J
Jewel 32, 35, 38, 55, 65, 84, 85, 86, 87
Johnson, E. Pauline 29

K
Kilcher, Jewel. See Jewel
L
Lakshmibai, Rani 101
Lhamo, Yungchen 46
Lilith, Mythical xii, xiii
Loeb, Lisa 22, 35, 63, 90
Lovelace, Ada 25
M
Malone, Michelle 45
McBride, Terry 21, 23, 26, 115
McClung, Nellie Mooney 93
McLachlan, Sarah
    and musical diversity 74
    and radio play 18
    and the press 32, 33, 42, 43, 65, 66, 67, 70, 71
    on adding men to Lilith 114
    on charities 30, 50
    on feminism 71
    on Lilith trial runs 22
    on sponsors 27
    opening for Sting 21
Meitner, Lise 73
Mudgirl 34
Multimedia
    and community 62, 63
    Lilith Web site 61
Music Festivals 11
    Another Roadside Attraction 14
    HORDE 14
    Lollapalooza 13, 14
    Michigan Womyn's Music Festival 12, 13
    Monterey Pop 11, 12
    Woodstock 11, 12

N
Nettmedia 61, 62
Nettwerk x
O
Osborne, Joan 42, 43, 87
P
Parks, Rosa 105
Persson, Nina 97
Planned Parenthood, controversy around 42
Press, The 66
        Ali, Lorraine 66
        Farley, Christopher John 65
        Ms. Magazine 71
        Powers, Ann 66
        Press conferences 32, 42, 43
        Time Magazine 65, 66
        Vowell, Sarah 67
R
Rasputina 34
Ray, Amy. See Indigo Girls
Role Models 3
        Fiona Apple on 53
        Jewel on 55
        Kim Fox on 55
        lack of 53
        Leah Andreone on 59
        negative 55
        Paula Cole on 58
Rolling Stone 15, 66
S
Saliers, Emily. See Indigo Girls
Scientists, Women
        Hypatia 69

        Lovelace, Ada 25
        Meitner, Lise 73
Senesh, Hannah 49
Shukibu, Murasaki 89
Sobule, Jill 46
Soldiers, Women
        Lakshmibai, Rani 101
        Senesh, Hanna 49
        Trung sisters, the 121
Stanton, Elizabeth Cady 37
Suffragettes 4
        Goldman, Emma 41
        McClung, Nellie Mooney 93
        Novel, First Written 89
        Stanton, Elizabeth Cady 37
        Wollstonecraft, Mary 81
Susanna and the Elders 17
T
Tale of Genji, The 89
Tekahionwake. See Johnson, E. Pauline
Trung sisters, the 121
Truth, Sojourner 117
V
Vega, Suzanne 15, 22, 32, 107
Vendors, selection of 31
Village Voice 66
W
Wild Strawberries, The 45
Williams, Victoria 109
Willis, Kelly 47
Wilson, Cassandra 44, 45, 78
Wollstonecraft, Mary 81

Buffy Childerhose is a full-time culture vulture and critic. She's currently the author of "Culture Swab," a culture column in Montreal's alternative weekly *Hour*, where she also serves as an editor at large. A veteran of film, fine art and creative writing programs, Buffy brought this melange to a graduate program in journalism where she proceeded to fuse the storytelling traditions of her family history to the business of journalism. A zine maker, editor, artist, poet, TV personality, producer, performer and hopeful novelist, Buffy wears enough hats that she could play milliner to a hydra. *From Lilith to Lilith Fair* is her first book.